SMIT.

DON PATERSON was born in Dundee in 1963. He is the author of *Nil Nil* (1993), winner of the Forward Prize for Best First Collection; *God's Gift to Women* (1997), winner of both the T. S. Eliot Prize and the Geoffrey Faber Memorial Prize; and *Landing Light* (2003), which won both the T. S. Eliot Prize and the Whitbread Prize for Poetry. *Rain*, his most recent collection, won the Forward Prize for Best Collection in 2009. In 2010 he was awarded the Queen's Gold Medal for Poetry. He has also published versions of Antonio Machado (*The Eyes*, 1999) and Rainer Maria Rilke (*Orpheus*, 2006), as well as two collections of aphorisms. He teaches at the University of St Andrews, and also works as a musician and editor. He lives in Edinburgh.

MICHAEL DONAGHY was born in the Bronx, New York, in 1954. In 1985 he moved to London, where he spent the rest of his life, writing, teaching and playing traditional Irish music. He died in 2004. Donaghy was the author of four volumes of poetry: *Shibboleth* (1988), *Errata* (1993), *Conjure* (2000) and *Safest*, which was published posthumously in 2005. His poetry received numerous awards, including the Geoffrey Faber and Forward prizes.

Also by Don Paterson

Poetry

Nil Nil

God's Gift to Women

The Eyes

Landing Light

Orpheus

Rain

Aphorism

The Book of Shadows

The Blind Eye

Best Thought, Worst Thought

Criticism

Reading Shakespeare's Sonnets

Editor (selected)

101 Sonnets

Robert Burns: Selected Poems

Don't Ask Me What I Mean *(with Clare Brown)*

New British Poetry *(with Charles Simic)*

DON PATERSON

SMITH

*A Reader's Guide to the Poetry of
Michael Donaghy*

PICADOR

First published 2014 by Picador
an imprint of Pan Macmillan, a division of Macmillan Publishers Limited
Pan Macmillan, 20 New Wharf Road, London N1 9RR
Basingstoke and Oxford
Associated companies throughout the world
www.panmacmillan.com

ISBN 978-1-4472-8197-9

Copyright © Don Paterson 2014
Michael Donaghy's poetry © Estate of Michael Donaghy 1988, 1993, 2000, 2005

The right of Don Paterson to be identified as the
author of this work has been asserted in accordance
with the Copyright, Designs and Patents Act 1988.

All rights reserved. No part of this publication may be reproduced,
stored in or introduced into a retrieval system, or transmitted, in any form,
or by any means (electronic, mechanical, photocopying, recording or otherwise)
without the prior written permission of the publisher. Any person who does
any unauthorized act in relation to this publication may be liable to
criminal prosecution and civil claims for damages.

1 3 5 7 9 8 6 4 2

A CIP catalogue record for this book is available from the British Library.

Printed and bound by CPI Group (UK) Ltd, Croydon, CR0 4YY

This book is sold subject to the condition that it shall not, by way
of trade or otherwise, be lent, re-sold, hired out, or otherwise circulated
without the publisher's prior consent in any form of binding or cover other than
that in which it is published and without a similar condition including
this condition being imposed on the subsequent purchaser.

Visit *www.picador.com* to read more about all our books
and to buy them. You will also find features, author interviews and
news of any author events, and you can sign up for e-newsletters
so that you're always first to hear about our new releases.

for Ruairí

Contents

Introduction ix

The Present 1
The Hunter's Purse 4
Remembering Steps to Dances Learned Last Night 8
Shibboleth 13
Caliban's Books 17
Held 22
Cruising Byzantium 26
The Brother 31
Acts of Contrition 35
Machines 40
Angelus Novus 43
Annie 48
Auto da Fé 51
The Bacchae 55
Cage, 59
Celibates 62
Where is it written that I must end here, 65
City of God 70
The Classics 76
A Disaster 81
'Smith' 84
Erratum 90
The Tuning 95
The Excuse 99

A Repertoire 103
Riddle 109
From the Safe House 113
Haunts 120
Disquietude 126
Local 32B 131
Hazards 136
Irena of Alexandria 141
Meridian 144
A Messenger 147
Not Knowing the Words 150
Our Life Stories 153
Pentecost 157
Tears 163
Timing 167
The Tragedies 170
Privacy 174
Ramon Fernandez? 178
Reliquary 185
The River in Spate 188
Southwesternmost 191
The apparatus 197
The Swear Box 200
Two Spells for Sleeping 203
Upon a Claude Glass 206
Exile's End 211

Introduction

Michael Donaghy was born to Irish parents, and grew up amongst the Irish community in the Bronx, New York. He studied at Fordham, and began a PhD at the University of Chicago. Becoming dismayed with academia (of his experiences at the time, he wrote 'gradually I became aware that professing English because I loved poems was like practising vivisection because I loved dogs'), he dropped out of the PhD programme to pursue a career in writing and in traditional Irish music. In Chicago he met his future partner, Maddy Paxman, and joined her in London in the mid-1980s. Here he spent the rest of his life, writing, teaching and playing music. In September 2004, Donaghy died of a brain haemorrhage. He was fifty years old. At the time of his death he had long been in the front rank of British poets, though his work remains inexplicably neglected in the US.

Donaghy published only three volumes of poetry in his lifetime: *Shibboleth* (1988), *Errata* (1993) and *Conjure* (2000). An early US publication, *Slivers*, was suppressed – though most of the poems in that book made their way into *Shibboleth*, his first collection with Oxford University Press. *Safest*, his final collection, was published posthumously in 2005. It was hastily assembled from the work he had left in a folder of the same name. As appropriate as we felt it to be, this didn't indicate his choice of the title: other folders containing less-finished material were marked 'safe' and 'safer'. These four volumes were gathered together in his *Collected Poems* (2009), together with some juvenilia and fugitive pieces. Except for a few uncollected squibs and disjecta membra, his life's work fits comfortably into a 240-page extent. Published at some little distance from his death, the *Collected Poems* offered us the chance to assess Donaghy's work more disinterestedly; his poetry stood stronger for not being quite so overwhelmed by his personality, and turned out to be far stranger, far more serious and far more complex than most of us recalled.

*

When Michael Donaghy died there was a carnival of mourning: 'well-loved' is an obituary-speak cliché, but never was it uttered more sincerely. At the time, this made the task of discussing Michael's work difficult, because all anyone seemed to want to do was talk about Michael – his kindness, his lightning-quick mind, his wisdom, his goofball humour, his good looks, the trail of (mostly) happy destruction he'd leave in his wake. He always had a strong inkling that his term would be cut short, and the poems are littered with clues and intimations; however, he compensated with some energetic living. A deadly mix of charm and vulnerability meant that, inevitably, a number of women – and a few guys – mistook the genuine and indiscriminate concern he expressed towards everyone for something more narrowly personal. Several seemed to think that they had drawn closer to Michael than anyone had before, often after only one or two encounters. This was a mistaken impression he will have been complicit in fuelling. Few knew him well, and perhaps only Maddy Paxman had any real understanding of the complexity of his personality, or the number and tireless imagination of his demons. But he had, as they say, a great gift for friendship: as a friend, he was deeply loyal and dependable (not to be confused with 'reliable', which was not a word anyone ever applied to him), and he would both light up and civilize any company he joined. Everyone seemed to love Michael – so much so that if you *didn't*, it might be considered a stain on your character. More than anything else, he was at great pains to make everyone feel safe, 'safe' being the one thing he rarely felt for himself. He never really stopped being a boy, in either appearance or behaviour, and I could never imagine Michael in his seventies. Neither, I am convinced, could he.

Michael's only fault was that he could be too forgiving. He loathed conflict of any kind, having seen too much of it in his childhood; he had a better sense than most that we have no time to indulge our recreational enmities. The worst name he had for someone was 'fool'. As the smartest of our number by some distance, this was still a pretty terrible judgement, and was reserved for certain poker-faced elements within the avant-garde, and those little critics who see poetry as nothing but an excuse to have a bitchy conversation about poets. As far as Michael was concerned, poetry was a force for enlightenment, for compassionate wisdom – and there was enough alienation, bitterness, cacophony and fragmentation in the world already without recruiting poetry, of all things, to contribute more.

I know several poets who will take no advice because they think they know exactly what they're doing. A few are correct, but most would benefit from thinking otherwise. We all lose perspective, we all suffer lapses of judgement, taste, intelligence and technique, and we are all our own blindspots. Michael was a genuine exception. I first met him at Colin Falck's poetry workshop in Hampstead in the late eighties; we were introduced through a close friend of his, my then-partner, the

American poet Eva Salzman. Donaghy was already something of a star, having won the Whitbread Poetry Prize with his first collection, *Shibboleth*.

In the workshop, Michael would thoughtfully nod at every suggestion, dutifully write down every comment, and thank everyone for their insight and assistance. In the four or five years we attended those meetings, I saw almost no evidence of him changing a single word as a result of anything anyone said.* He was there for the craic, and little else. As well as his friend for fifteen years, I was Michael's editor at Picador, after the OUP list folded. Trying to edit Michael was pretty much a waste of time. I don't doubt he'd have listened if I'd had anything sensible to contribute; but his poems were always wholly finished, perfectly balanced and interlocked constructions, like those self-supporting wooden bridges built without nails or bolts, and held together by nothing but the genius of their own engineering. He would occasionally concede the odd comma, but only, I suspect, out of pity. I would invariably find that he'd reinserted it in the proofs. Of recent poets, I can think of only two or three who possessed his ability to work a poem's elements into such a convincing unity.

Charisma – which Michael had in abundance – tends to be one of the loudest qualities we can possess, and it often simplifies the work. It's also a volatile quality, and usually burns off within a year of the death of the author, when we're then free to move on to biographical distortions. Charisma in the quantity and concentration Michael had it, alas, is more of a

---

* He did, I recall, change the title of 'Held' on someone's inspired suggestion. 'That's *much* better. That's *so much* better . . .' he said, shaking his head in disbelief at having missed it.

problem, because it suffuses the work itself. Too many still think of Michael's work as merely elegant, charming and witty, since these are the qualities it most obviously embodies. His poetry is certainly all those things. But Michael was also possessed by fear, guilt, insecurity, paranoia, fatalism and a deeply buried anger, and these are inscribed in the work too. Far more significantly, the poems are evidence of an exceptional literary intelligence. The fact he managed to get so many of these poems past us as 'entertainments' was in itself a miraculous confidence trick.

Partly, his motivation was neurotic. We all want to be loved, but Donaghy made sure of it. He was a hilariously funny and spellbinding performer, who would always recite from memory, reasoning that if he couldn't remember his own poems no one else was likely to either. The poems, too, are performances, designed to entertain first; but *what* your mind had been asked to entertain was something else again. Often it turned out to be a far stranger guest than the one who'd turned up all hail-fellow-well-met on the doorstep. Donaghy's aim was always to hit the temporal lobes and the solar plexus simultaneously, but the lower blow is always landed first: sometimes the visceral punch or sheer entertainment value was so strong, a reader might be inclined to defer the poem's intellectual pleasures indefinitely. These complexities are often further disguised by Donaghy's Frost-like ability to make densely nuanced arguments through very simple language and statement. (I should add that his poetry was occasionally dismissed – and, I suspect, will continue to be – by that class of critic who can only acknowledge the existence of complexity when it has announced itself in what they feel is language of appropriately commensurate difficulty.)

Most of his poems start with a dramatic proposition that makes it almost impossible not to keep reading on: '*Hair oil, boiled sweets, chalk dust, squid's ink* . . .' 'What did they call that ball in *Citizen Kane*?' '"My father's sudden death has shocked us all." / Even me, and I've just made it up'. Like Frost, he sounded light, but read dark. This requires not only an extraordinary technique, but one selfless enough to disguise every trace of its own labour, and often of its own ferocious intertextuality. He trusted the reader and respected their intelligence, even if he knew that was likely to mean playing a longer game. True, he wrote many set pieces; as funny, sharp and lyrical as they all were, they were not his best work, even though he often favoured them at readings. These poems reflected his trickster tendencies: he delighted in pranks played on the reader – riddles, jokes and not-so-buried puns. While a few of those pieces are discussed here, I have concentrated on what I feel were Michael's major poems.

For years I had been aware of vaguely troubling cracks, flaws and discontinuities in those poems which I'd either skated over, or set aside for a later I never quite got round to. In much contemporary poetry, what looks like a loose end is often exactly that. Here's not the place to debate the merits of the discontinuous or fragmentary style: it has both increased the possibilities of the poetry we can write and the kind of thought and experience poetry can reflect. It has also provided much cover for incompetence and charlatanry. In Donaghy, a discontinuity – isn't: you've merely failed to understand something. Those patterns of cracks, I should have realized earlier, were just the shape of my own ignorance. They have since opened up readings that have seen one poem after another unfold and bloom into unsuspected dimensions.

Time and again I would get my nail into one of these tiny abysses, apply a bit of pressure – and watch as the poem suddenly clicked, swivelled and opened up like a Chinese box. Inside, there is almost always something astonishing and beautiful, or demonic and unwelcome.

Donaghy refused to operate under any of the usual flags of convenience, and saw himself simply as an Anglophone poet who took the best from traditions on both sides of the Atlantic. His early influences were Hopkins, Pound, David Jones and Charles Olson (though Olson soon got the heave, and swiftly became something of a bête noire). Borges was less an influence for Michael than a neural rewiring, one which changed everything that followed. Borges supplied him with a model of textual dimensionality: an understanding of how, through the careful selection and interdependence of every single detail, three quarters of a poem's meaning could be embedded in a kind of semantic harmony, while taking up no more space on the page. The Elizabethan poets and the poetry of Paul Muldoon gave him the structural models to accomplish this; while Donaghy's voice and rhetorical strategies are very different from Muldoon's, the complex-yet-inevitable relation of the part to the whole was learned from him. He was obsessed with (and wrote a fine long poem about) Benvenuto Cellini and the animatronic golden birds in Yeats's Byzantium poems. His own poems, too, are exquisitely crafted things, beautifully tooled, self-winding mechanisms.

The poets who made his voice were all those he memorized: Donne, Marvell, Herbert, Shakespeare, Keats, W. B. Yeats, Robert Graves and Louis MacNeice; then the US poets whose work he read within the English lyric tradition – Dickinson, Eliot, Bishop, Lowell and Frost (he seemed to have half of Frost by heart, and I suspect he'd have traded him for most of the others). The vocal influence of Muldoon, Longley and Heaney is present in his work, but critics overstate it. Derek Mahon, whose work he adored, made the stronger impression, as did the rhetorical courtesies of the US 'old formalists' Richard Wilbur, Anthony Hecht and James Merrill.

I believe that the best of Donaghy's poetry stands up against almost any of them, and that's what I hope to convince you of here. All this book will do is talk about fifty of his poems in an open-ended, unmethodical fashion, although I have titled each short piece to give some indication of my critical focus from poem to poem – and, I hope, emphasize the various and multifaceted nature of Donaghy's work. I suspect, too, that this is the closest I'll get to writing a 'how to read a poem'-type book; but because I don't think anyone really needs or wants such a thing, it's really just a book about the way *I* read poetry, or at least read Donaghy. There are many ways to 'do criticism'. The only wrong ways are those which find things which aren't there, those which supply more mud than clarity, those which claim to supply 'correct' readings (of which there can be none), and those which claim a fundamentally superior critical methodology. I am not really a literary critic, just a poet who reads poetry. The very best poet-critics rise to the occasion of each poem by forging a shape of equivalent or superior wit and intelligence, but that's neither my competence nor my purpose. Nor is it to do the one thing I *can* do with reasonable skill, and give a technical analysis of the poetry, although I will certainly raise a few points of interest along the way. My intention is simply to explain these poems a little, give some account of their depth, power and complexity, and discuss the ideas and feelings they prompt. I have also given them some biographical and personal context. Some of my readings will be plain wrong and others will disagree with your own. This is just as it should be: poems are half-said things, and have no solutions, only readings. (My readings are also too uncritical – lord knows I probably should have been harder on his almost-demented Fibonacci obsessions, which will certainly test your patience – but for obvious reasons, I have concentrated on his best work here.) It was my original intention to reprint each poem immediately after my notes, in an attempt to force you to read it twice. This was a pretty wasteful *and* patronizing scheme, so I'll substitute it with a plea: read this book however you like, but do read each poem again following my comments. You'll find it changed a little, and sometimes a great deal: none of Donaghy's poems read the same way the second time round, and how they end almost invariably rewrites them.

As will already be clear, Donaghy was a man I knew well and loved dearly, and I have not attempted to disguise the fact. For this reason, some may find this book uncomfortably personal and too dissonant with their idea of useful criticism. Perhaps they're right, but any other reading would have been a dishonest one. To deny what we know of the author in our reading of their work is to suppress both their humanity and our own, and I've no interest in reading poetry as if it were – to adapt a phrase of Randall Jarrell's – written by a typewriter, for a typewriter. I am, however, aware of the pitfalls of my too-close acquaintance with the author. Donaghy's work will require a less improvisatory and conversational analysis than I've provided in this book, and his life a far less sketchy and dewy-eyed account than I have given here (though in the meantime, readers could do far worse than turn to Maddy

Paxman's fine memoir *The Great Below*). Still, I hope I've cleared a little ground so the work can begin, because there is a great deal of it to do. These poems do not 'repay rereading': they demand it, and were constructed on that principle by a phenomenal literary intelligence, and a man cursed with an almost Rilkean knowledge of the tragic and paradoxical nature of our being.

I am greatly indebted to the friends (many of whom were also close to Spike) who took the trouble to read this text and suggest changes, and I'd like to thank Nora Chassler, Ian Duhig, Paul Farley, Nick Laird, Eva Salzman and Greta Stoddart for their invaluable input, as well as Maddy Prior and all the gang at Stones Barn. I'm especially grateful to Maddy Paxman, who offered many personal insights, corrected several factual errors, and pointed out several sins of both commission and omission.

This book is for Michael's son, Ruairí Tomás, on the occasion of his eighteenth birthday.

SMITH

The Present

For the present there is just one moon,
though every level pond gives back another.

But the bright disc shining in the black lagoon,
perceived by astrophysicist and lover,

is milliseconds old. And even that light's
seven minutes older than its source.

And the stars we think we see on moonless nights
are long extinguished. And, of course,

this very moment, as you read this line,
is literally gone before you know it.

Forget the here-and-now. We have no time
but this device of wantonness and wit.

Make me this present then: your hand in mine,
and we'll live out our lives in it.

Time and distance

This sonnet makes a fine wedding poem, and I wish it were more widely employed. It'd certainly be a lot more appropriate to that fraught occasion than 'Let me not to the marriage of true minds / Admit impediments', which really only works well at a civil partnership between two gay men, one of whom is in jail. But this, in its way, is also an Elizabethan sonnet – with its air of formal disquisition, in its metaphysical concerns, and through its carefully elaborated conceit, invoking the moon, that old 'lozenge of love', to explain something of the real nature of time. (It also has a slightly archaic courteousness, and later tips its hat to Walter Raleigh.) Its form is a 'disguised Italian': the ABAB CDCD EFEFEF rhymes indicate the usual octave + sestet arrangement, but it's laid out in couplets, possibly as an echo of the romantic union it finally declares as its real subject.

The two meanings of 'present' are beautifully conflated in the final couplet: the gift of the lover's hand is also a tense in which one can live. The first line is a great place to slip one past the reader, who generally isn't paying full attention yet. *For the present there is just one moon* means, I suspect, 'there is one moon for the time being, in the lives that we currently enjoy on our monosatellite earth', with a hint of 'but who knows near what star we may be reborn?' While there may be only one moon orbiting the earth, the laws of optics see it multiplied everywhere, on every still and reflective surface. But light isn't transmitted instantaneously, and it takes a while to hit our retinas from its source. The light from the reflected moon takes milliseconds to get to us, and the moonlight itself

1.7 seconds to get to the pond – and the light from the sun seven minutes to get to the moon, before the moon can reflect it. When the moon disappears, we can better see the starlight, much of which has taken thousands, millions of light-years to reach our eyes; so long, in fact, that many of the stars we see are now burnt out and gone from the night sky, which is less a real thing than a very long, slow film of our long-dead ancestors.

But never mind those stars. The problem is far closer to home. By the time you read the words *gone before you know it*, the previous line, *this very moment . . .* is already in the past. That the past is not a 'real thing' is something humans are hardwired to deny; yet it's nothing, and it does not exist. But time doesn't really 'do' the present either. All passes, incessantly; there *is* no *here-and-now* to contemplate. *Wantonness and wit* is from Raleigh's 'Nature that washed her hands in milk' ('. . . and had forgot to dry them'), a familiar Elizabethan riff on beauty vs time, delivered with unfamiliar brilliance:

> Her eyes he would should be of light,
> A violet breath, and lips of jelly;
> Her hair not black, nor overbright,
> And of the softest down her belly;
> As for her inside he'd have it
> Only of wantonness and wit.

We have no real time but the strange clock of our inner being. *We* are the device of wantonness and wit, of free play and of free intelligence. And all we have to close the gap between image and source, between past and present, is each other, in our bodily forms.

The Hunter's Purse

      is the last unshattered 78
by 'Patrolman Jack O'Ryan, violin',
a Sligo fiddler in dry America.

A legend, he played Manhattan's ceilidhs,
fell asleep drunk one snowy Christmas
on a Central Park bench and froze solid.
They shipped his corpse home, like his records.

This record's record is its lunar surface.
I wouldn't risk my stylus to this gouge,
or this crater left by a flick of ash –

When Anne Quinn got hold of it back in Kilrush,
she took her fiddle to her shoulder
and cranked the new Horn of Plenty
Victrola over and over and over,
and scratched along until she had it right
or until her father shouted

   'We'll have *no* more
   Of *that* tune
   In *this* house to*night*'.

She slipped out back and strapped the contraption
to the parcel rack and rode her bike
to a far field, by moonlight.

It skips. The penny I used for ballast slips.
O'Ryan's fiddle pops, and hiccoughs
back to this, back to this, back to this:
a napping snowman with a fiddlecase;
a flask of bootleg under his belt;
three stars; a gramophone on a pushbike;
a cigarette's glow from a far field;
over and over, three bars in common time.

History

This is perhaps the best of Donaghy's 'ethnomusicological' poems. The earliest wave of US Irish immigrants were especially proud of their occupations, and would declare them at every opportunity – as was the case with the great tune-collector Police Chief Francis O'Neill, the author of *Irish Folk Music: A Fascinating Hobby, with some Account of Related Subjects*, whom Donaghy wrote about in a poem called 'The Reprieve'. In pointedly telling us Anne Quinn hails from Kilrush, Donaghy makes a quiet but interesting point: yes, it was an unqualified good that recording facilities available in the US allowed the playing of so many fine musicians to be preserved, but when these records were shipped back to Ireland, they confused regional styles. O'Ryan's Sligo is nowhere near Kilrush in Co. Clare; so Anne will have learned the song in the Sligo style, a bouncy, faster fiddle style than the slower, less decorated 'lonesome touch' of her local Clare fiddlers. The result was a stylistic cross-pollination and miscegenation that wouldn't have otherwise taken place.

This record's record is its lunar surface refers to the secondary 'record' Anne Quinn made of her own presence, imprinting it on her copy of O'Ryan's original 78, the moon to the original's sun. She played it to death – Donaghy would ham up the father's lines 'We'll have *no* more / Of *that* tune / In *this* house t*onight*' quite wonderfully at readings – and it's clearly a mess of scratches and cigarette burns.

In this record's record's record, the poem itself, we see the stuck 78 collapse time and space. He can't keep the needle on the shellac: Anne Quinn's fag-burn left such a bad gouge that it skips, and skips. But behind the repeated phrase, he finds the whole story in palimpsest: O'Ryan's scratchy old fiddle; O'Ryan dead with his fiddlecase; the booze under his belt; three stars above the moonlit field in winter; Anne, with her mad double contraption of bike-and-gramophone; the star of her cigarette-tip in the dark field; over and over and over, in the endless cycles of our linked experience. All condensed into the same three bars of reel-time, repeating endlessly. 'Common time' is just the 4/4 time signature, but here also puns beautifully to stand for the time music allows us to share across decades, and the entire collective enterprise.

One hopes the poet looked after this last unshattered disc better than Anne Quinn, though we needn't worry, since it never existed. Anne may have lived, or may have not – but you'll have clocked by now that there was never a Patrolman Jack O'Ryan. *One snowy Christmas* was supposed to alert us to the fact that the story was always too good to be true; when he recited the poem, Donaghy always leaned heavily on *snowy*, so we'd get it. The poet even told us straight, but we weren't paying attention the first time. He was indeed 'a legend', and no more. Two legends, indeed: 'Jack Orion' is the man with the enchanted fiddle in the traditional ballad: 'But he would fiddle the fish out of salt water / Water from bare marble stone / Or the milk from out of a maiden's breast / Though baby she had none . . .' And Orion, the great Hunter, whose tune this is. Those *three stars* at the end make up O'Ryan's Belt, where Jack tucked his flask (possibly there's also reference to Orion's blinding, after Dionysus had got him blind drunk). His reel, like his constellation, is real enough. The stories of where we got our tunes are some of our best; since no one can remember, they might as well be.

Remembering Steps to Dances
Learned Last Night

Massive my heart, the heart of a hero, I knew it,
Though I was ten, pimpled, squint eyed, dung spattered.
I strung a bow, and memorized a brief heroic song
(I'll sing it for you later), left my goats in my father's yard,
And then went down to the ship.
Many men massed at the dock, loud their laughter.
But the king listened, noted my name, gave me wine,
A little patriotic speech, and sent me home
To the goats and the tedium and the ruminant years.
Once I made a song about the king and his distant plundering
And the hoard of memories, wondrous, he was gathering.
It's a shame you didn't bring your guitar.

Then one summer, when I was older,
And the king was long since missing in action,
Men came from Achaia to court the lonely queen.
The nights got loud with drums and laughter echoing from
 the palace,
Women's laughter, and the smell of roasted lamb.
What would you have done? I pounded on the gates one
 morning,
Rattled my arrows and stamped and sang about my hero-heart.
They seemed to understand . . . Or didn't mind my lying,
And they opened the gates on another world.
Beauty. Deception. Of weaving, of magic, and of the edge of
 the known world
When the light fails, and you fall dead drunk across the table,

All these we learned in our feasts and games amid the grey-eyed women.
Clever men and many we waited, the queen to choose among.

I know you came to hear me sing about the night the king came home,
When hero slaughtered hero in the rushlit hall,
Blood speckling the white clay walls wine dark.
I can't. I'd stepped outside when the music stopped mid-tune.
Alone in the dark grove, I heard no sound but distant insects,
And the sound of water, mine, against the palace wall.
And then I heard their screams, the men and women I'd spent that summer with.

What would you have done?
I staggered home in the dawn rain, still half drunk,
Forgetting one by one the names of my dead friends,
Remembering steps to dances learned that night,
that very night,
Back to my goats, goat stink, goat cheese, the governing of goats.

The hero's tale

Donaghy was an acquaintance of the great comparative mythologist (and fellow Irish American) Joseph Campbell. Donaghy never shared his enthusiasm for Jung's theory of archetypes, but was drawn to Campbell's idea of a 'monomyth' that lies behind all others; this was often referred to in his work as 'the hero's journey'. (Donaghy loved Graves's 'To Juan at the Winter Solstice': *There is one story and one story only / that will prove worth your telling* . . .) He was just as strongly compelled to reject it: I feel he might have had Campbell in mind, here, with this little anti-myth that falls determinedly outside that narrative. This is the kind of story *not* refined in the wind-tunnel of the oral tradition, *not* told round the hearth by generation after generation. But it's this guy's only good story, and tell it he will. And he does so beautifully.

This dramatic monologue is spoken by a drunken goatherd. Despite the 'low' and deliberately Anglo-Saxon language he uses, he is, we soon learn, one of the unseen extras from Homer's *Odyssey*, a character so insignificant that he was cut long before the final edit. His tragedy, his goat-song, is that his *hero-heart* was never and will never be expressed; by the time he tells his tale he has long resigned himself to the miserable life of *goats, goat stink, goat cheese, the governing of goats*, the life he returns to at the end of the poem.

The poem opens with his attempt to join Odysseus's ship as a ten-year-old boy; but he's been born too late, and has quite literally missed the boat. (l.5, *And then went down to the ship*, is cheekily stolen from the first line of Pound's *Cantos*, itself a version of the passage in the *Odyssey* where Odysseus journeys to Hades to speak with Tiresias.) While the boy is laughed at by some, the great king treats him with an indulgent kindness – and sends him back to his goats: *ruminant years* is a resigned pun. He composes a song about the epic he has missed out on. He has the touch of the drunken poet-bore about him, and is a little too fond of the sound of his own voice: *It's a shame you didn't bring your guitar.*

Anonymous for years, our little goatherd suddenly rejoins the story when Penelope's dissolute and greedy suitors have moved onto the absent Odysseus's estate. Here they enjoy free wine, food and board while they wait for the queen to choose a replacement for her long-presumed-dead husband. She is stalling for time, weaving and unweaving her tapestry. Understandably, our ambitious goatherd wants in on all this action, and somehow his silly song about his hero-heart gains his admission into the palace. The other world he learns of within its walls is just as unheroic as his own, but at least it's glamorous – and compared with the ignominy of his usual situation, feels like the hard-partying hub of things. Who knows? Perhaps if things had gone differently, our man might have had a chance with the queen herself.

The one song that would have been *really* worth hearing – he *can't* sing. He was out the back taking a leak when Odysseus and Telemachus stormed the halls, and for an hour it was all hero-on-hero action of the sort he'd spent his life dreaming of. Which just about sums it all up, really. All he heard was the music stop; the sound of his own water . . . And then the screaming. Wouldn't we have done the same? The right, drunken, cowardly thing – forget the names of your murdered friends, and dissolve into the dark? All he has to remember his time with them by is a silly little dance he learned that very night, the only thing that will survive of the dreadful killing hall.

The title seems wonderfully lyric on first reading, but it's really bitterly pathetic and bathetic. The poem is too strong to be 'merely what it's about', and takes on real allegorical force: the hero's tale doesn't even have a tiny role for us, and the great lives we wish for are often mercifully denied us.

Shibboleth

One didn't know the name of Tarzan's monkey.
Another couldn't strip the cellophane
From a GI's pack of cigarettes.
By such minutiae were the infiltrators detected.

By the second week of battle
We'd become obsessed with trivia.
At a sentry point, at midnight, in the rain,
An ignorance of baseball could be lethal.

The morning of the first snowfall, I was shaving,
Staring into a mirror nailed to a tree,
Intoning the Christian names of the Andrews Sisters.
'Maxine, Laverne, Patty.'

Identity

Most people now use 'shibboleth' to mean a slogan or a catchword, but it was originally more of a password; the failure to pronounce it correctly would reveal you as an imposter or persona non grata, and swiftly lead to your death. The word means either 'ear of corn' or 'flood stream', though the latter is likelier, given the original context:

> *And the Gileadites took the passages of Jordan before the Ephraimites: and it was so, that when those Ephraimites which were escaped said, Let me go over; that the men of Gilead said unto him, Art thou an Ephraimite? If he said, Nay; Then said they unto him, Say now Shibboleth: and he said Sibboleth: for he could not frame to pronounce it right. Then they took him, and slew him at the passages of Jordan: and there fell at that time of the Ephraimites forty and two thousand.*
>
> Judges, 12

There have been many such tests. The most notorious of recent times was perhaps the one used in the so-called 'Parsley Massacre' in the Dominican Republic in 1937; the then-president, the unspeakable Rafael Trujillo, asked his troops to identify Haitian immigrants living along the border by asking that they say the Spanish word for 'parsley', *perejil*. Through their inability to do so in the Dominican manner, between 20,000 and 30,000 Haitians were murdered within a few days. Which again reminds you that there's really nothing on this earth so small, trivial or innocent that humans can't contrive to hang a genocide on it.

In the south-east-Asian theatre in World War II, Japanese soldiers approaching American checkpoints were asked to say 'lollapalooza', which their l/r allophone makes very difficult to accommodate: anything close to 'rorraparooza' would be met with a burst of gunfire. In Troubles Ulster, the alphabet itself would suffice. On reaching the eighth letter, *haitch* or *aitch* would indicate either a Catholic or Protestant upbringing, at which point things might be swiftly decided one way or the other. The situation was given a grim twist, since the interviewee often had no idea whether their interrogator was IRA or UDA; second-guessing the 'right' answer could be either the luckiest guess you'd ever made, or pointlessly dangerous.

The occasion Donaghy probably had in mind here was the Battle of the Bulge in World War II, when US soldiers famously used baseball trivia to reveal German infiltrators. ('Snowfall' would be right, as the battle was fought between December '44 and January '45). Though this is a poem not just about paranoia, but identity too. How do you *demonstrate* you're you? *Are* you you? The speaker here is, apparently, a GI who feels he must rehearse his *own* authenticity in case he is mistaken for an infiltrator. The poem lists those who failed, and ends with the frightened rehearsal of the kind of silly thing by which the authentication of one's Americanness might hang; one, we can be sure, of millions.

On a second reading, though, *we're* recruited to the ranks of the paranoid. Name Tarzan's monkey: Cheetah. (*Cheater*? Anyway what kind of name is that for a monkey?) And hang on a minute . . . Why does the speaker refer to a 'GI' if he *is* one himself? Note, too, how the middle stanza works from both a German and a US perspective. *The second week* in the Battle of the Bulge would have been Christmas season. I wonder what The Andrews Sisters' big hit was that month? I make it 'There'll be a Hot Time in the Town of Berlin'. Snow, Christ, trees, nails; the crucified self in the mirror . . . in which he sees *who*, exactly? We can't know if this man is for real, and perhaps he can't either. Incidentally, he also misspells 'Maxene'.

Caliban's Books

Hair oil, boiled sweets, chalk dust, squid's ink . . .
Bear with me. I'm trying to conjure my father,
age fourteen, as Caliban – picked by Mr Quinn
for the role he was born to play because
'I was the handsomest boy at school'
he'll say, straight faced, at fifty.
This isn't easy. I've only half the spell,
and I won't be born for twenty years.
I'm trying for rainlight on Belfast Lough
and listening for a small, blunt accent barking
over the hiss of a stove getting louder like surf.
But how can I read when the schoolroom's gone
black as the hold of a ship? Start again.

Hair oil, boiled sweets . . .
But his paperbacks are crumbling in my hands,
seachanged bouquets, each brown page
scribbled on, underlined, memorized,
forgotten like used pornography:
The Pocket Treasury of English Verse,
How to Win Friends and Influence People,
Thirty Days To a More Powerful Vocabulary.

Fish stink, pitch stink, seaspray, cedarwood . . .
I seem to have brought us to the port of Naples,
midnight, to a shadow below deck
dreaming of a distant island.
So many years, so many ports ago!

The moment comes. It slips from the hold
and knucklewalks across the dark piazza
sobbing *maestro! maestro!* But the duke's long dead
and all his magic books are drowned.

Spells

This rich, complex and terribly sad poem attempts and fails an impossible task: to raise and comfort the dead. Three stanzas of uneven length are each prefaced by a kind of spell-making or invocation. (They make thirty lines in total, echoed in the title of *Thirty Days To a More Powerful Vocabulary*.) The poem describes a lineage of magickers: not the line of Prospero, the unjustly usurped Duke of Milan, but of Caliban, with whom Donaghy aligns himself. (See *my people were magicians*, from 'The Excuse'.) The magic books referred to in the title are not the kind Prospero owns, but books of self-transformation, which might instruct the beast in the arts of self-improvement – and turn him into something other than the animal he knows himself to be.

Donaghy was forever raising the ghosts of his beloved dead. The poem starts with a spell to summon his father from his schooldays in dirt-poor Belfast. (His father left school at fourteen, but he was a dedicated autodidact who shared his son's interest in esoteric philosophies.) *Hair oil, boiled sweets, chalk dust, squid's ink* . . . With these period touchstones, he's trying to invoke his father's schoolroom, the place where his dreams of a transforming education began. Who knows if his father was joking when he said that the reason Mr Quinn cast him as the hideously deformed Caliban was that 'I was the handsomest boy at school'? He's keeping a straight face. Do we read this as more evidence of his father's uneducated boorishness, or was he winding up the young poet?

The scene the poet invokes is steadily overwhelmed by the sea of *The Tempest* – the sea which also bore his father far from home. *I'm trying for rainlight on Belfast Lough* . . . Belfast Lough is the gateway into the Irish Sea; the blunt barking Ulster accent of his father's schoolmaster is heard over water boiling on the stove – but within this sound he hears the roaring surf, and all is suddenly drowned in the sea-journey. The spell fails, and the schoolroom turns dark *as the hold of a ship*. The storm is gaining hold.

We try again with the same spell. *Hair oil, boiled sweets* . . . But we've moved on. The magic books of his father's which may have prompted the spell-making in the first place – *How to Win Friends and Influence People*, *Thirty Days To a More Powerful Vocabulary* – are falling apart. No wonder: they're not the gold-tooled Moroccan-bound grimoires of Prospero, but old mass-produced paperbacks, used beyond use. The allusion in *seachanged bouquets* brings us back to *The Tempest*, via the poem's own paternal subject. Ariel tries to comfort Ferdinand for the loss of his father to the sea's depths: *Full fathom five thy father lies, / Of his bones are coral made, / Those are pearls that were his eyes, / Nothing of him that doth fade, / But doth suffer a sea-change, / into something rich and strange.* Although Caliban's magic hasn't worked. The lessons, such as they are, have been memorized but then forgotten. 'Used pornography' is an odd phrase, but emphasizes the abject shame of his father's enterprise.

The poet's next spell is very different: darker, older, seaborne. *Fish stink, pitch stink* . . . What is the poet trying to conjure here? And where are we now? The play is long finished. Prospero has been freed by the acclaim of his audience. His ship has long sailed away from the enchanted island back to Naples. But poor, pathetic, knuckle-dragging Caliban is now back in Naples too, having somehow boarded a ship as a stowaway (in this passage there are strong echoes of another below-decks-island-dreaming-monster, King Kong). He hopes that he will find Prospero, his 'schoolmaster', who will, perhaps, finally initiate him into the ways of wisdom and social sophistication. But not only does he find the Duke *long dead*; all the books by which he could *effect* such a transformation are destroyed too – just as he had promised at the end of the play.

What's the island Donaghy's father-Caliban dreams of? The old homeland, Ireland, the enchanted isle of his early confinement and lowered expectations. Naples is New York; the journey there, as it was for most immigrants, was an aspirational one. But his father lost himself somewhere between exile and misplaced ambition, and in the end finds himself terribly led astray, with no teacher, and no home at all.

Held

Not in the sense that this snapshot, a girl in a garden,
Is named for its subject, or saves her from ageing,
Not as this ammonite changed like a sinner to minerals
Heavy and cold on my palm is immortal,
But as we stopped for the sound of the lakefront one morning
Before the dawn chorus of sprinklers and starlings.

Not as this hieroglyph chiselled by Hittites in lazuli,
Spiral and faint, is a word for 'unending',
Nor as the hands, crown, and heart in the emblem of Claddagh,
Pewter and plain on that ring mean forever,
But as we stood at the window together, in silence,
Precisely twelve minutes by candlelight waiting for thunder.

Timelessness

Poetry doesn't really do complex structure. It *thinks* it does, sometimes, or at least poets think they do – but compared to the novel and the philosophical essay, the narrative, litanic, argumentative or discursive forms that almost all poems take are relatively simple. (The few exceptions – Merrill's *The Changing Light at Sandover*, for example – are generally novelistic in both scale and shape.) Our sophistications tend to lie less in the architecture of the poem and more in the subtlety with which its elements interrelate. Just so here: the structure is simple, but the *way* the evidence works together to build the poet's case is anything but. This poem has the lightest of schemes: *not this, not this, but that; not this, not this, but that*. Not 'held' in *that* sense – but in *this*.

Our usual ideas and symbols of timelessness, eternity, 'forever' – are not in themselves timeless at all. The truly timeless 'held moment' escapes time entirely. The two moments Donaghy declares here as authentically 'atemporal' are, crucially, shared – and shared between those who 'held' each other closest: lovers. Is this the only way we can experience no-time? When our own limits, the clocks of our own solitary minds, are dissolved by another's presence?

So: not *held* as a pose is held for the camera, which then holds it 'forever' in the Polaroid; not like a fossil; not like an ancient device the Hittites used for *unending*; not like a token exchanged to promise eternal love . . . No, those things aren't eternal. Not only are they objects in time, they merely *symbolize* the eternal, not realize it. I recall Donaghy citing with approval a Joseph Campbell lecture he'd attended. Campbell was pouring scorn on someone he'd heard try to explain the near-eternity of the cosmos: 'Imagine a bird flying over a mountain once every hundred years; every hundred years it pecks off one grain of earth. Well think of the length of time the bird takes to reduce the mountain to nothing. To the universe, that's a merest blink of the eye . . .' 'Bullshit,' Campbell had said. He snapped his fingers. '*That's* eternity, right there.'

The eternal moments he describes are two 'befores'. He and his lover cover the waterfront before life starts, before the birds, before human activity. The sound of the lakefront is the sound of nothing, of white noise, Donaghy's mark-of-the-great-beyond. (What are these two doing up so early? Have they been to bed yet?) The second little eternity takes place in the evening, before *thunder*. There's a punchline quietly buried in this final scene that one might miss: the poet is trying to recall this treasurable moment accurately, but he fails. When is one *waiting for thunder*? After lightning. You count off the seconds to measure how far away the storm is. But in this infinitely precious moment, there *was* no time to count: the best he can do is convince himself he counted off *precisely twelve minutes* between the flash and the report. Of course this can't be true; but love, as we saw in 'The Present', has little time for time.

Donaghy being Donaghy, there is one more riddle to be discovered. Twelve minutes may echo both the twelve lines in this beautiful poem and the clock face it has frozen. In which case we have, at the very least, a delightful coincidence – though I strongly suspect it was deliberately placed. How far away was the lightning? Divide the number of seconds by five to get the answer in miles: $12 \times 60/5 = 144$ miles. The number 144 is the twelfth Fibonacci number, and the square of twelve;* it's the number of the chosen in Revelation, the height in cubits of the wall of New Jerusalem, and so on; it's a sacred number associated with complete cycles, wholes, the eternal.

This is a highly unusual form, comprised of twelve lines of triple metre, arranged as two six-line stanzas. Each consists of three couplets, which themselves are composed of a line of five strong stresses followed by one of four, giving an almost ballad-like space for breath at the end of each couplet. (Another way of putting it would be to say that it's a 26-syllable strophe with a strongly overdetermined dactylic feel.) The beautiful exception – we must always remember Donaghy's love of echoing or enacting his theme in the form itself – is the final line, which also has five strong stresses, and was held for longer than you thought.

---

* There are also twenty-one (a Fibonacci number) solutions to the equation $\varphi(x) = 144$; $\varphi(x)$ is Euler's totient function, which is all about relative primes and which I barely understand, so let's not go there. I mention it only because Donaghy might well have known all this. I am assured he took a similarly esoteric approach to his tax returns.

Cruising Byzantium

The saved, say firemen, sometimes return,
Enduring the inferno of the flat
To fetch the family photos. And they burn
Not for cash, cashmere coat, nor cat,
Nor, as they momently suppose, for love.
They perish for the heraldries of light
And not such lives as these are emblem of.
But the saved, say firemen, are sometimes right.

Have you seen our holiday snaps from Greece?
Each Virgin burns in incandescent wonder
From her gold mosaic altarpiece.
This one was smashed by Gothic boot boys under
Orders from an Emperor who burned
The icon painters for idolatry.
Before her ruined face the faithful learned
The comet's path to a celestial sea.
And look. Here's *you* in skintight scuba gear
Winking through the window of your mask!
You have become the fetish that you wear.
I know precisely what you're going to ask;
Though golden in the Adriatic haze
You've waded to your thighs in molten light,
Your second skin aglitter in the sprays,
Your first it was we brought to bed that night.
And yet I'd almost brave the flames to keep
This idyll of perversity from burning.

Each photo frames a door beyond which, deep
Within the Patriarchate of my yearning,
The marble pavements surge with evensong.
But firemen say the saved are sometimes wrong.

The Beyond

This is a beautifully subversive piece of writing, deeply entangled with the world of Yeats's two classic poems, 'Byzantium' and 'Sailing to Byzantium'. This poem is in what some might call a 'strict' form, though it's so effortlessly achieved one would be forgiven for not noticing. The three uneven stanzas disguise a thirty-line iambic pentameter ('i.p.', hereafter) poem of successive quatrains, almost perfectly full-rhymed ABAB, with a closing couplet. Its brilliantly mongrel tone is declared immediately in the title, with its 'high' proper noun and 'low' qualifier, announcing the poem's project of revealing a timeless classical world behind the quotidian. Yeats's poems also engage with this world-outside-time, beyond or weirdly collateral with our own: a world in which there is no 'becoming', but only 'being'.

Donaghy proposes that we regard our treasured snapshots as both intimations of and gateways to this timeless place, and *that's* the reason we might die for them – not for who they represent. The first eight lines are clear enough. We've heard the stories, though I have no idea if they're true: the house is ablaze, but everyone has made it outside to safety; then someone foolishly goes back inside to retrieve the photo albums, and they're done for. The poet says: no, they're *not* going back to stage a symbolic rescue of those they love or have loved – more often we *don't* die for love – but for the idealized representations of what love is: the fetishized image *itself*, not the person it depicts. And then we have a line that should give us pause. *But the saved, say firemen, are sometimes right.* Hang on: firemen literally *never* say that. So why does the poet? I think because the *firemen* here are not just the red-engine-and-yellow-hose variety. They are also Yeats's *sages standing in God's holy fire* whom he wishes to be *the singing-masters of my soul*, and then gather him *into the artifice of eternity*. 'The saved' are both those saved *from* the fire and *by* the fire. They're *right* to enter the purifying flames again.

In the second, longer part of the poem, we see the two worlds collide and interfuse. The poet compares two kinds of icon – one people really did die for, and one Donaghy proposes they *might* die for. It starts with an unexpectedly chirpy and conversational line: *Have you seen our holiday snaps from Greece?* Donaghy then introduces his Byzantine theme more explicitly: *gold, fire, emperors*. The first holiday snapshot is of an icon of a gilded Virgin, set in a gold mosaic altarpiece; here, we're asked to think of *the gold mosaic of a wall* from which Yeats's holy firemen emerge, an image very much from the world of timeless being. Here's another one, damaged, smashed up by some Ostrogoths on the orders of one of those iconoclastic Byzantine emperors of the seventh or eighth century (most of whom, incidentally, seemed to marry women who were secret iconophiles; the period is long overdue some serious Freudian attention). Icons worth dying for, clearly.

But *this* one? Very much from the down-and-dirty here-and-now, the world of becoming, we're shown a snap of the poet's lover in scuba gear, looking like she's on fire as she wades out into the golden light of the Adriatic. What *does* the poet know, precisely, that you're going to ask? You're going to ask . . . 'Would you *die* for this image of me? Would you enter the fire to salvage this idyll of purifying fire from a real blaze?' Maybe he would. A bold touch is his suggesting that this rubber skin is worth more that the *real* one he takes to bed –

or at least this image of it is. The rubber makes it fetishizable, something that can be worshipped as an *idyll of perversity*, a secular icon of transforming and eternal desire that would also be worth dying for.*

The final stanza says that each of those beloved 'held' and timeless moments of frozen, burning desire is a portal: a door into true being, to a timeless Byzantium. (A *patriarchate* is a Byzantine see or province; *the marble pavements surge with evensong* is another direct reference to 'Byzantium'.) Surely it's worth it to brave the flames, and retrieve these magical icons in which the visions of the beyond are held? *But firemen say the saved are sometimes wrong.* This line dumps us back in the 'real' world again, with those solid, helmeted, hosed-up fireman, holding you back and telling you not to be bloody ridiculous . . . All this Byzantium stuff, alas, is nothing but a consoling dream; the world of becoming, passing and dying is all there is. The kids and the cat are safe. It was only a photograph, so let it burn. But then again . . . Maybe the saved are sometimes right.

---

* Like many poets, Donaghy was very taken with the distinction Roland Barthes makes between 'punctum' and 'studium' in *Camera Lucida* (his peerless short book on the photographic image), and gave a great deal of thought to how it might relate to the poem. The 'studium' refers to our broad interpretation of the image in the context of what we know of its social, political or cultural provenance; the 'punctum' is the strange, 'wounding' detail, the tiny odd little thing in the photo we end up fetishizing, and the conduit of our personal feelings toward the image itself.

The Brother

Dropping a canapé in my Beaujolais
At some reception, opening or launch,
I recall briefly the brother I never had
Presiding at less worldly rituals:
The only man at my wedding not wearing a tie;
Avuncular, swaddling my nephew over the font;
Thumbing cool oil on our mother's forehead
In the darkened room, the bells and frankincense . . .
While the prodigal sweats in the strip-lit corridor.

Now, picture us facing each other, myself and the brother
I never met: two profiles in silhouette,
Or else a chalice, depending how you look.
Imagine that's this polystyrene cup.
I must break bread with my own flesh and blood.

Ambiguity

This is, quite deliberately, a *perfectly* ambiguous poem. It starts with two lines that, if you read them too quickly, might appear to describe an act of metropolitan sophistication – but the silly triple assonance of *canapé / Beaujolais* alerts us to the presence of comedy. Slapstick, even: the speaker is a putz, a clumsy guest, and he's accidentally dropped his reheated M&S mushroom vol-au-vent into his wine. This, it later transpires, is being drunk from a polystyrene cup. (Never overestimate the glamour of the literary do; publishing is a kind of skint showbiz.) However, this little accident initiates a train of thought that steadily leads to something like a personal devastation. Donaghy is not averse to shaking up the tone, and in some ways this is the poem's secondary project: to show that our bleakest realizations can be prompted by the most trivial or comic things.

The poem addresses a sense of personal inadequacy that goes well beyond mere lapsed-Catholic guilt, and into a whole other realm of self-disgust and sodden disenchantment. His wine/canapé disaster immediately alerts the speaker to the symbolism of the bread and the wine, and the fact that this book launch or prize-giving is a *worldly ritual*, a secular rite. Immediately he introduces his central paradox: he recalls someone who never existed. (The title may nod to 'Christian Brothers', but I suspect Donaghy had in mind Flann O'Brien (writing as 'Myles na gCopaleen') and his permanently off-stage character 'The Brother'. The Brother is never seen, but his great works are reverently reported: he is, we gather, a man of phenomenal knowledge, ability and political influence.)

He slyly alerts us to his identity. Who is the only man at a wedding not wearing a tie? I like this little riddle, because it briefly sends you off in precisely the wrong direction before it clicks. Oh yes: the same one who also baptizes the child, and reads the mother her last rites. The more important point is that, in each case, the poet has been usurped. This priest-twin is *avuncular*, which is a deliberate and clever redundancy on Donaghy's part: if he's the poet's brother, he *is* also the uncle of the baptized child. The *nephew* is the poet's, but his religious double is the one really fulfilling the avuncular duties. As the prodigal son, he is banished from being present at the last rites of his own mother, which his brother conducts. (Donaghy's mother had ambitions for him to join the priesthood, and his never-brother is that road not taken.)

This is a lopsided sonnet in very loose, unrhymed i.p. (though some lines – the penultimate, for example – are fairly tight). It breaks 'wrongly' between lines 9 and 10, rather than taking the conventional Italian volta between 8 and 9; possibly this echoes the theme of 'wrong breakings' that the poet introduces later in the poem. In the last stanza Donaghy contrives a miserable but brilliant trick: a triple pun, with its precise visual analogue in an old optical illusion, which he now proceeds to flip, flip, and flip again. Picture the two of them, in facing, identical profile. Then the picture changes, and instead of two silhouettes, you see a vase – or in this case, a chalice. A chalice, because what is summoned between their two profiles is a sacrament, a holy ghost who can intercede where the poet cannot, and can conduct the communion. However, the chalice the two brothers conjure up is a poor one, since one brother is a fiction. Imagine the chalice is this polystyrene cup, full of cheap booze and floating bits of pastry. The tawdry bathos is crucial here. As an unbeliever, *I must break bread* ('share deeply' and 'take communion') in whatever worldly circumstances I find myself. But having summoned my brother by invoking the chalice, I can break it with him, since he's family: *my own flesh and blood*. But once the illusion switches and becomes the chalice . . . the brother disappears. *My own flesh and blood* is now merely literal, and refers to nothing but the brotherless, three or four cubic feet of flesh, bone and blood that I am — if I'm to commune with anyone at all, it's with myself, because there's no one else here. However, the bread and the wine are also the *flesh and blood* of Christ in the Holy Communion: I am using my own flesh and blood *as* the sacrament. I'm consuming myself, changing my own blood into wine. And look at me; just look at the state of me.

Acts of Contrition

There's you, behind the red curtain,
waiting to absolve me in the dark.
Here's me, third in the queue outside
the same deep green velvet curtain.
I'm working on my confessional tone.

Here's me opening my wrists
before breakfast, Christmas day,
and here's you asking if it hurt.
Here's where I choose between *mea culpa*
and *Why the hell should I tell you?*

Me again, in the incident room this time,
spitting my bloody teeth into your palm.
I could be anyone you want me to be.
I might come round to your point of view.

Confessional poetry

Donaghy's sonnets were often so well disguised it was easy to miss them: this is just how the poet desired it, and their 'sonnetude' is often the least interesting thing about them. This poem is something of a home game for Donaghy, and puns on three interpretations of the word 'confession': the Catholic confessional, 'confessional' poetry, and the legal confession of guilt.

Most good poems can be relieved of much of their apparent difficulty by asking the four big questions of literary deixis: *when is this? where are we? who are these people?* and *is this supposed to be real?* Establish the tense and the order of events, the location, and the identity of the pronouns, and you're halfway there. In poetry we have a further thing to clarify, partly because we so often work in allegory and metaphor: by *is this real?* I mean 'is the described event mimetic of a reality, or something that takes place in an imaginary or figurative space?' (Literary 'realities' don't have to be *true*, of course — only read as if they were.)

Where? Well, in the first stanza, the confessional box; in the second, probably a hospital, in the aftermath of a suicide attempt; the third, the incident room after his arrest. When? The poem is written in the present continuous, a tense we sometimes use to describe past events in a 'timeless' way, as if we were never free of them. Who? In the first, the *you* is established as the priest, and we can then reasonably assume it's the priest throughout, or at least someone in that father-confessor role. Finally, there's no cue that we are to take these events other than literally.

The speaker is in the queue for confession, and he's rehearsing his 'confessional tone' – in other words, about to commit an act of total insincerity. The curtain is double-sided, and that red will come up again soon. The 'you' behind the hellish red curtain is monstrous; as the poem progresses, the speaker is being led by his interrogator towards his own blood, which will finally authenticate his sincere confession. Right now, all the priest wants to hear – with feeling – is the Catholic act of contrition:

My God, I am sorry for my sins with all my heart. In choosing to do wrong and failing to do good I have sinned against you whom I should love above all things. I firmly intend, with your help, to do penance, to sin no more, and to avoid whatever leads me to sin. Our Saviour Jesus Christ suffered and died for us. In His name, my God, have mercy. Amen.*

In the second stanza, having almost committed the sin of suicide that carries the penalty of damnation – the priest-figure is showing the poet some concern, or at least some attention. (We may decide that there's some causal link between

---

*   Maddy Paxman tells me that Donaghy would always confess to the sin of anger, knowing it was the one he could not have committed. He grew up in a household that was both violent *and* loving, but had seen enough fighting to last him a lifetime. (As his namesake Jack Donaghy says in the TV show *30 Rock*, 'The Irish mate for life, like swans. Like drunk, angry swans.') As a result, he was a kind of walking Switzerland, which could prove immensely frustrating. He would only confess his real enemies – or tell you what he *really* thought of your poem – after a fair few drinks.

the stanzas, and that his own suicidal desperation is in itself connected, somehow, with his earlier refusal to comply.) He is being asked again for his contrition – but there's no guarantee the priest will get the *mea culpa* he wants; the poet swithers between an admission of guilt and another refused confession, a 'get lost'.

However, the second stanza is also about the 'confessional poet' at work. 'Confessional poetry' was the name given to the 'poetry of oversharing' we associate with John Berryman, Robert Lowell, Anne Sexton and Sylvia Plath, and their accounts of their very real mental illnesses, bad relationships and addictions. The word 'confessional' was first applied in this way by the critic M. L. Rosenthal in 1959 in his review of Lowell's *Life Studies*; the confessional mode came with a subject line which read For Your Too Much Information, and in Rosenthal's words 'went beyond customary bounds of reticence or personal embarrassment', removing the conventional literary persona that hid the real face of the poet. (The black private 'joke' here is that Donaghy really *is* writing confessional poetry, and is double-bluffing. He made just such a suicide attempt as a young man, and was discovered by luck, not design. He doesn't, however, consider this an important enough detail to explicitly 'share' with us.)

Maybe his interrogators need to take a stronger line? Here we are again, this time in the incident room of a police station. The speaker is being beaten up, we can now assume, so he will make a confession. It seems this will finally result in the sincerity demanded by his interrogator. And they win in the end: *I could be anyone you want me to be.* The last line is something of an arch luxury, under the circumstances: *I might come round to your point of view.* He clearly has every intention of doing so. 'Auto da Fé', the title of another Donaghy poem, means more or less the same thing: a penance and confession that would be tortured out of you. It's not enough to be sorry. We have to be sorry in the prescribed manner, otherwise the official order is upset. And we usually can, given sufficient incentive.

Machines

Dearest, note how these two are alike:
This harpsichord pavane by Purcell
And the racer's twelve-speed bike.

The machinery of grace is always simple.
This chrome trapezoid, one wheel connected
To another of concentric gears,
Which Ptolemy dreamt of and Schwinn perfected,
Is gone. The cyclist, not the cycle, steers.
And in the playing, Purcell's chords are played away.

So this talk, or touch if I were there,
Should work its effortless gadgetry of love,
Like Dante's heaven, and melt into the air.

If it doesn't, of course, I've fallen. So much is chance,
So much agility, desire, and feverish care,
As bicyclists and harpsichordists prove

Who only by moving can balance,
Only by balancing move.

Argument

This is the sort of poem that won Donaghy the reputation of a 'modern metaphysical'. There's no doubt that Donne, Marvell and Herbert were among his primary influences, though Donaghy's later poems will often conceal their sometimes complex algebraic form. The first line declares two things: firstly, that this is a love poem; secondly, that its thesis will be delivered with some authority. The mock-formal, didactic address is maintained throughout.

The poem is about neither harpsichords nor bikes, but the love-poem itself . . . Only we don't know that yet. The bike and the harpsichord pavane aren't obviously alike at all, however, so the poem has that *Oh do go on* . . . quality. Then we're given the solution: *the machinery of grace is always simple*. Except there's nothing particularly simple in either example, so the statement merely intrigues us further. This graceful, perfect machine of interconnected gears was how Ptolemy imaged the solar system to be; the idea was rubbish, alas, as Copernicus later demonstrated, but it was a lovely vision. However, that vision was realized otherwise in the wonderful geared machine created by F. W. Schwinn, whose father Ignaz founded the Schwinn Bicycle Company in Chicago at the end of the nineteenth century. Either way, the bike is gone, and the cyclist has pedalled off; that's what a good bike does – disappear. In the same way, the pattern of Purcell's pavane, his dream-machine of interconnected notes, is played out of its own existence, as the harpsichordist plays away the blueprint of the written score. But there's a little more to it than that.

We get to the heart of the poem with a second comparison. *This* very talk, this poem, this little love-speech I'm giving right now – something I could translate into the sense of touch, if only I was physically closer to you – works in the same way. Read it, and it will do its love-work, and then be gone, like the nine spheres of the *Paradiso* wherein Dante's beloved Beatrice resides. (The *Paradiso* ends with Dante figuring how these spheres all work together, and concludes that it's through God's love: *Here power failed my lofty vision / But now my desire and will were turning / like a fixed wheel rotating evenly / by the Love which moves the sun and the other stars.* While Donaghy puts it all somewhat more concisely, behind both poems lurks the idea of *musica universalis*, the celestial geared wheels and Pythagorean ratios that govern the harmony of the spheres.) If it doesn't, I've failed as a poet – I've fallen off the bike, or I've hit the cracks, and I have proved a lousy operator of my own poem-machine. I've tried, though, with all the *feverish care* I've put into this love-speech, driven by my own desire for you . . . But in the end, it all comes down to this real-time performance, in which movement and balance depend perfectly upon one another; if they can't, both bike and cyclist fall over, and the musician (as musicians say) 'falls off the chart'. So how did I do?

I think he knows the answer. Since the balancing act here *is* the poet's elaborate comparison . . . Is this really a love poem, or just a poem *about* a love poem? Like many of Shakespeare's sonnets, it appears to be more about poetry than love; however in both cases, I think love is expressed less in the content, which says very little about the beloved, than in the gift of the near-perfect poem itself – which says everything.

Angelus Novus

As in this amateur footage of a lynch mob when
someone hoists a metal folding chair and commences
to batter the swinging corpse even as others hack at
its limbs with machetes, just so Achilles, his frenzy a
runaway train, yokes up his team and drags Hector's
carcass around and around like . . . Stop. Rewind.

Hector dying on his knees in the dust whispering
*Prove you're a man, then, swear by your soul, swear by
your gods you won't feed my corpse to your dogs.*

Fuck you spits Achilles. Freeze frame. Mid-blink,
Hector looks into Achilles' eyes and takes all the time
in the world to recall his last embrace of Andromache
and, it hardly now surprises him, to look back at
the future advancing behind him, to his own father
kissing the hands of this killer, the monster taking
Priam's hand and weeping with him, the sound of
their sobbing filling the camp. Play on. Hector's face
slams to the dust.

Try to look at this: blind flash victims. Nagasaki. In
their endless 1945 they face the camera as unaware of
the photographer as they are of you, viewer. Just so,
rage-blind Achilles cannot now glimpse in Hector's
eyes, just before they empty, the terrible pity.

Perspective

Donaghy was obsessed with perspective in all its forms. In a less grim mode, he once described Uccello's own perspectival obsessions in a poem *about* the dangers of obsession: *Her personal vanishing point, / she said, came when / she leant against his study door / all warm and wet / and whispered 'Paolo. Bed.' / He only muttered, / gazing down his grid, / 'Oh, what a lovely thing perspective is!' / She went to live / with cousins in Madrid.* ('Lives of the Artists', part II: 'The Discovery and Loss of Perspective').*

The title of this four-part prose poem refers to the Paul Klee painting of the same name, and riffs on Walter Benjamin's well-known description of it. Benjamin saw Klee's huge-headed, bird-like figure as a kind of 'angel of history', who perceives time not as a linear succession of events but as

> one single catastrophe which keeps piling wreckage upon wreckage and hurls it in front of his feet. The angel would like to stay, wake up the dead, and make whole what has been broken. But a storm is blowing from Paradise; it has got caught in his wings with such violence that the angel can no longer close them. The

---

* Paul Farley tells me that he heard Donaghy read this poem to a particularly drunk and raucous audience in Liverpool, and when he got to the final line 'She went to live / with cousins in Madrid', he heard a voice out of the darkness say: *Good*. This was also the evening that someone, post-performance, told Michael he was in love with himself (a career in psychoanalysis perhaps did not beckon), to which he flashed back: 'But d'ya think I'll go all the way?'

storm irresistibly propels him into the future to which his back is turned, while the pile of debris before him grows skyward. This storm is what we call progress.

We have been killing each other for ever. Perhaps one reason we do so is that we have no real vantage, and see each murderous episode as just one event in a disconnected series, each with its own local justification – rather than a single great atrocity which swells with the passing decades. Here, we jump-cut between several horrors as though they were aspects of the same. The poem opens with the horrible scene of what sounds like an African or Deep South lynch-mob, where the already-dead victim is being hacked to pieces, and battered with whatever random object comes to hand. Then we cut to a scene of similarly murderous fury from the *Iliad*, where Achilles, not content with putting Hector to the sword, will desecrate his corpse and drag it behind his chariot. The poet uses the language of cinematography (the whole poem is about visual record) to *rewind* to an earlier moment, where Hector begs him to respect his corpse, and leave him whole for burial. Despite his begging, Achilles is pitiless.

Then the poet stops time in a freeze-frame. Now we see that in the exact moment of death, Hector has the angel's terrible perspective. He looks ahead, and recalls his last embrace with his wife (who will be taken as a concubine by his enemies, while their son is killed); then he looks *behind* him, and stares into the future, where he sees his proud father King Priam forced to abase himself while he begs Achilles for the return of his son's carcass. This is supposed to sound odd: nowadays, we'd turn *back* to the past and look ahead to see what's coming – but like the angel, Hector's future is behind him. 'To look into the future' would have been an entirely different conceptual exercise for Hector: the Greeks – and, we can assume, the Trojans – sensibly believed the future lay behind them, not before them, since they couldn't see it. (The inversion of this sensible directional metaphor strikes me as fundamentally symptomatic of our appalling hubris: of course we can't see what's coming. To think that we *can* leads to actions which are, by any sane standards, reckless and blind.)

The poet hits *play*, and Hector falls dead. Now we fast forward. The flash victims of the Nagasaki bomb are indeed difficult to look at: they were flayed as well as blinded by the flash. The look in their eyes is frozen to the vanishing point of their own blinding. Is *this* what the eyes of the dead looked like at the instant of their dying – like Hector's, suddenly sharp with the angel's eternal perspective? They are filled with pity for the entire species, one condemned to repeat its atrocities and enormities for ever, learning nothing. *We* are the rage-blind Achilles, unable to see for our own low and animal anger. What's the moral here? Santayana famously said (let's give the quote in full for once), 'Progress, far from consisting in change, depends on retentiveness. When change is absolute there remains no being to improve and no direction is set for possible improvement: and when experience is not retained, as among savages, infancy is perpetual. Those who cannot remember the past are condemned to repeat it.' But the truth is that we remember the past just fine, and then go and repeat it anyway. The answer, the poet seems to be saying, lies in false ideas about the nature of time (an interpretation reinforced by many other poems in which Donaghy makes the same argument). What we need to adjust is our relation not to history, but to time itself, and to perspective itself. The corpses mount and mount. We are deluded about the nature of physical law; time flows, and does not separate us from our actions in the way we think. Clear of this delusion, we might then see the single unbroken atrocity that has accompanied our time on Earth like a lengthening shadow.

Annie

Flicker, stranger. Flare and gutter out.
The life you fight for is the light you kept.
That task has passed this hour from wick to window.
Fade you among my dead my never-daughter.

Upriver in your mother's blood and mine
it's always night. Their kitchen windows burn
whom we can neither name nor say we loved.
Go to them and take this letter with you.

Go let them pick you up and dandle you
and sing you lullabies before the hob.

Elegy

This is one of the few poems I know almost *sadder* than an elegy; at least the elegized got to exist. Despite the best efforts of the three parties concerned, this child just couldn't find the foothold or handhold that would gain her a secure grip here. But though her flame wouldn't take, the brief candle of the child's life isn't the end of her light – only of her light *here*, on this gravity-bound planet, where we cup it in our bodies for a while. That fight for life has passed (*this hour* speaks of a specific passing; one doesn't want to intrude upon the privacy of the parents to enquire further), but the task of keeping her light is merely transferred from *wick to window*, from the individual body to the wider sky . . . Which the poet suggests is fading with the arrival of night, and into which the child must now venture alone. But while it may be dark outside, there's still warmth and safety to be sought.

Upriver in your mother's blood and mine is the ancestral source of the long dead. Most of us can't remember our great-grandparents' first names. We never loved them, yet we're rooted in their having existed. Donaghy tends to use the imperative mood to command just as fate or natural order commands: here, it's the instruction for this never-daughter to take the letter of introduction – the poem itself, heartbreakingly – to those kindly yet unknown family members. The word 'hob' is a signifier of the rural, and takes us to an Irish hearth, a place of warmth where things can be kept alive. ('Hob' is cognate with 'hub', if you go back far enough.)

Here, Donaghy's technique disguises every trace of itself: excepting one or two more rhetorically formal lines, the pentameter is so naturally achieved you might not notice it, mainly because the poet almost didn't either; for poets of Donaghy's expertise, i.p. is a motor skill. Woven through the poem almost obsessively are consonantal chimes: *flicker/ flare; gutter/daughter; fight/light; task/passed; fade/dead; never/ upriver; mother's/mine; neither/name.* The vowels are beautifully varied, but often arrive in assonantal pairs – *stranger/ flare; life/fight; task/passed; wick/window; never/daughter; mother's/blood; name/say* – so that one word never really feels alone, just as the child will not.

Auto da Fé

Last night I met my uncle in the rain
And he told me he'd been dead for fifty years.
My parents told me he'd been shot in Spain
Serving with the Irish volunteers.
But in this dream we huddled round a brazier
And passed the night in heated argument.
'El sueño de razón . . .' and on it went.
And as he spoke he rolled a cigarette
And picked a straw and held it to an ember.
The shape his hand made sheltering the flame
Was itself a kind of understanding.
But it would never help me to explain
Why my uncle went to fight for Spain,
For Christ, for the Caudillo, for the King.

Ignorance

We think of *auto-da-fé* as referring solely to the burning at the stake suffered by medieval heretics, but the 'act of faith' originally referred to the penance that took place before it. Here, its meaning is obscure, like so much of this poem – but then the poem is also obscure to the poet. The title may refer to the punishment his uncle is enduring, or it may just explain what lay behind his actions. This encounter is dreamt by the poet; if we accept his word that his uncle really *is* fifty years dead, we can date the poem to the late mid-1980s.

El sueño de razón . . . refers to Goya's famous etching 'El sueño de la razón produce monstruos' – 'The Sleep of Reason Produces Monsters'; Donaghy cheekily omits the 'la' to help his metre. In a typically nested, self-similar way, this also refers to the very dream the poet is having. In Goya's picture, the sleeping artist is surrounded by the wayward bats and dumb owls of error and ignorance. In his own dream, the poet finds himself no wiser. Goya's painting referred to what he saw as a deranged and corrupt Spanish society. When reason sleeps, there's trouble – as the imagination is then allowed to indulge its talent for unnatural, insane and unfettered creation.* And so here.

The poem ends with its punchline: his uncle had fought for the Caudillo – for Franco, not the republicans. There may

---

* *El sueño* can mean either 'dream' or 'sleep', and there's controversy over whether Goya intended 'when reason sleeps, monsters are produced' or 'the dreams of reason produce monsters'. For all I love academic debate, it's often addicted to the non-existent crux. Since be some truth behind this tale. I vaguely recall Donaghy telling me of some cousin or great-uncle of his who *had* indeed fought in Spain in the civil war; but his parents had conveniently withheld the fact that he'd gone to fight for the fascist cause, for Franco and the Nationalists, not the communists – probably with the pro-Catholic, anti-communist Blueshirts. This news would not be the sort of thing a fourteen-year-old kid in the Bronx with a Mao poster on his bedroom wall necessarily wanted to hear about his family, and it was kept from him. The Catholic Church was on Franco's side, and the war was fought for a Catholic monarchy. But history judges Franco as the soul who should be damned here; the White Terror took many more lives than the Red. This new information about his uncle was received to Donaghy's great dismay, since he'd been dining out on the better version of the story for some time.

The uncle appears to be literally burning, either in his own private hell, or in echo of the terrible judgement his own church inflicted on its dissenters. This lyric, delicately written, spaciously plain-speaking sonnet has a fascinating rhyme scheme, or rather 'rhyme scheme', since only ten lines really rhyme; the remainder 'rhyme' semantically, being various kinds of fire: *brazier, cigarette, ember, flame.* (It's odd that this hasn't been more widely imitated – it's tricksy, to be sure, but it does allow the quiet introduction of a little meta- or infra-poem for anyone who goes looking for it, and beats the hell

---

Goya's full motto for his etching is 'Imagination *abandoned* by reason produces impossible monsters: united with her, she is the mother of the arts and the source of her wonders' (my italics), his intention seems clear.

out of an acrostic.) These reinforce the sense that the 'heated argument' may be taking place where fire is the principal element.

To *pick a straw* – any straw – is also to abandon reason, and hand one's fate over to chance. *Why* did he do it? *For Christ, for the Caudillo, for the King*. It was a principled stand, whatever it was; should we see both sides of the story? The answer still makes no sense to the poet. *What* kind of understanding was vouchsafed, as his uncle cupped the flame to light his cigarette? Was it a gesture of secrecy? Did his uncle see himself as a kind of martyr? Was he a 'keeper of the flame', of the one true faith – or of the fires of hell, on which that faith depends? *Is* this hell? So many questions; but then reason is asleep.

The Bacchae

Look out, Slim, these girls are trouble.
You dance with them they dance you back.
They talk it broad but they want it subtle
and you got too much mouth for that.
Their secret groove's their sacred grove –
not clever not ever, nor loud, nor flaunt.
I know you, Slim, you're a jerk for love.
The way you talk is the what you want.
You want numbers. You want names.
You want to cheat at rouge et noir.
But these are initiated dames –
the how they move is the what they are.

Slang

If Dashiell Hammett and not Euripides had written *The Bacchae*, it might have gone a bit like this. Check them out, over there at the other end of the bar: crazy and beautiful, all glad rags, warpaint and dirty laughs – and looking like the best night out you'll have in your life. But *how they move is the what they are*. This isn't put on for your benefit. These are *initiated* dames – and you, friend, are not part of that inner circle. If you want to break into it, the choice is yours, but you've been given plenty of notice.

This is a reasonably straightforward poem, so forgive me a little technical diversion. There are really only two kinds of metrical line in English. You can have a line with four strong stresses, or you can have iambic pentameter, and that's the whole show. This may sound nuts, but all I can say in this short space is a) it's true, and b) I know because I've written a very long and boring technical paper on the matter which almost killed me. I accept that this argument has little force, but I'm currently suffering from the overweening self-confidence of the too-well-briefed, so please trust me for now. This poem is written in the four-strong line that lies behind many of the older oral and 'received' forms, including the ballad, trimeter, the hymn, the limerick, the Burns stanza, the 'dolnik' and even the English hexameter (it's a long story). Unlike the i.p. line, the four-strong line emerges directly from our habit of alternate stress, the so-called 'tick-tock' effect: because of this, we impose hierarchical patterns of alternating stress on any series of identical, close and evenly spaced events. This form arises naturally from our bodies, and has been around for ever. It instinctively makes us feel we're listening to something drawn from an oral and anonymous tradition, rather than a literary and authored one. This poem consists of three stanzas of what I (and others) call the 4×4 form, making a kind of 'oral sonnet' exquisitely appropriate to its racy, colloquial speech. There's a delicious frisson between the 'low' form and its classical subject, and it would make a fine country-and-western song.

At the point we enter the story, a stranger is addressing the hapless Pentheus, King of Thebes, and warning him off his urge to check out the crazed followers of Dionysus, the Bacchae. He says . . . 'You know what you want – and they have it, alright: the gen, the low-down, the inside story . . . But you're a klutz, and you don't know how to play them. These women are *trouble*.' *You want numbers. You want names* has two functions: it means both 'you'd like to find out who these women are, then date them' – but also ties the dialogue to the noir detective novels of the thirties and forties.

The stranger, alas, is Dionysus in disguise, who wishes to punish Pentheus for his earlier refusal to worship him. Despite the apparent sincerity of his cautions, all he's *really* doing in this speech is baiting the hook. Who *wouldn't* wanna hang out with these crazy gals? (After this exchange is over, and despite the warnings, Pentheus insists on getting closer. Following the stranger's advice, he disguises himself as a woman; the stranger helps him up to what Pentheus thinks is a safe vantage on the top of a fir tree, where he settles down for a leisurely gander. Suffice to say things do not go well, and the story ends with his own mother ripping his head off.)

The sparkling surface of the language is the main pleasure here. The speaker is very much drawn from hard-boiled central casting, but given to a kind of effortlessly brilliant, rather outrageous wordplay — *Their secret groove's their sacred grove* — that suggests a god not taking his own earthly appearance too seriously. And if gods have such things, his conscience should be clear: this is nothing if not fair warning.

Cage,

The composer, locked in a soundproof room in Harvard
Heard his heartbeat and the sound of Niagara Falls
Produced by the operation of his nervous system,
From which he derived a theory, no doubt.

Me, I heard a throaty click at the end of 'wedlock'.
And Niagara on the long-distance line.
I knew a couple once, went up there on their honeymoon.
After a week, they said, you don't even hear it.

Analogy

Hilariously, this was written as a commission for Valentine's Day. (Radio 4 rejected it on the reasonable grounds that it did not exactly meet the remit, and Donaghy offered them a clever squib about tattoos, 'Liverpool', instead.) The title is immediately and pedantically qualified: *Cage – the composer . . . in case you were confused by my intentions here*. But of course it's deliberately disingenuous. Since the poem hasn't started yet, titles happen in a kind of context-free space, which means that they're still unstable enough to propose a number of different senses; a lot of one-word titles pun – and Donaghy has another sort of 'cage' in mind too. John Cage did indeed hear white noise in the anechoic chamber at Harvard. He heard both high and low sounds; the low was his blood, the high his own nervous system. It takes a very quiet and muffled little cage to hear this constant Niagara, of which we're usually unaware. Cage is then rather snottily dismissed by the speaker of the poem – no doubt he *did* derive some theory (and he certainly got at least one iffy poem out of it), though it should be noted that John Cage had Donaghy's respect, whatever the rather sneering tone of this speaker.

White noise (it's technically 'pink noise', in this instance, but let's not split hairs) is a Donaghy signature. As we'll see, it usually indicates 'the beyond' – the world of no-time, pure being, of infinite possibility, the Byzantium that lies beyond both human perception and human existence. 'Possibility' is the key here, because that's exactly what the speaker feels himself denied. By what? In 'wedlock' he hears the turn and click of that *lock* very loudly and the cage bolt shut behind him. This poem is the song of the terminal commitment-phobe. As soon as he signs himself over to another, the Niagara of the self starts receding, and his nervous system, the means of his sentient feeling, is now calling long distance: white noise at the end of the line indicates there's no one there.

The Niagara Falls, a traditional honeymoon destination in the US, are never louder than when we're right next to them. And we're perhaps more attuned to ourselves and to our own nervous systems when we're in love than at any other time, because we're so wakefully attentive to each another, and all that. But after a week of *wedlock*, the poet seems to claim, this great Romantic tumult, this vast noise of possibilities . . . is all but gone. You get used to it. You can't hear yourself at all, as the other person is drowning you out. Indeed you're about to hang up on yourself, and you may never hear from you again. Welcome to your *cage* . . .

Celibates

They're closing down the travelling fair this week.
The crystal balls are packed, the last sword swallowed,
and the geek has shaved and caught the night bus home.
Beyond the dimming generator lights we stick it out,
blind masters of the dying arts, by night, by winter rain,
squatting in the rotting straw of our cages.
The recordreader strokes a disc and snaps back
Gould, *The French Suites*. The booksniffer naps,
face pressed to the uncut pages of the life of Keats
that he has just inhaled. The last haruspicator
snacks on hay with the phrenologist whilst I perform
another brilliant twist in the Meran Variation
of the Queen's Gambit! History, made, fades away
unseen – as interest in exhibition solo chess
has markedly declined. But you, you inspire us,
frighten us, with your extraordinary abstinence,
obscurity and silence. Only a soft chittering
tells me you're there now, naked, knitting,
with tweezers, small flames – dark gold flash
of brass foil, spring coil, and gear – into tonight's
unsold array of clockwork crickets.

Obsession

I think it's less the idea that makes this poem than the hyperbolic intensity of its expression. Celibates? Remember them? You hardly ever see one these days. Of all the performers in this travelling circus, they're the strangest. Most of the weirdos the poet mentions in this 21-liner (yes, it's the F-word again) certainly existed: entrail-readers, crystal-gazers . . . 'recordreaders' really *could* identify a specific recording from the pattern of grooves on a 78; the booksniffer I'm less sure about, though Donaghy used to claim he could identify a publisher by the smell of the glue on the binding. Either way, the whole gang – the fakes, the freaks, the fortune-tellers – are heading from mere obscurity into total oblivion. The little circus is closing down, and the sword-swallower and the geek have disappeared into that freak's oubliette known as normality.* (A 'geek' was originally a kind of fairground stooge; here he sounds like the Amazing Dog-faced Boy, or similar.)

Ducking playfully in and out of something like i.p., the speaker describes his own dying art last: that of solo chess. (Solo chess is a theme that emerges in another Borgesian poem of Donaghy's, 'A Sicilian Defence'.) He's so brilliant a player that he casually makes chess history – which immediately passes away unrecorded. Solo chess-players are, you sense, worryingly close to the celibates the speaker professes to

---

* Todd Browning's *Freaks* was a favourite film of Donaghy's, and this poem shows its clear influence. Another is *The Break*, which is partly about Daisy and Violet Hilton, the conjoined twins who starred in Browning's film.

admire and fear. But none of this can match them for wilful obscurity. Their trick or shtick seems to be just keeping themselves to themselves, but to a quite superhuman degree; those anchorites of the flesh are almost invisible in their deranged self-containment.

The tiny strange trinkets that the celibates produce – through their viciously channelled sexual frustration? – are unvalued and unsold. They are knitting the little flames of their desire, manifest as slivers of brass foil and clockwork innards, into meticulously complex little models no one wants. The gilded mechanical animal is one of Donaghy's obsessions, a complex symbol that can be traced both to Yeats's Byzantium poems and to Benvenuto Cellini. It stands for something like both pointless *and* transcendental perfection and artifice. I confess I'm not quite sure what this poem is saying, other than that celibacy – which the speaker seems (tellingly) to regard as the absolute withdrawal of oneself from human circulation – is a perverse and purposeless thing, and perhaps no virtue; but nor is it deserving of our derision. But by 'celibacy' I suspect he simply means the isolation created by any form of truly obsessive behaviour. It may be an allegory about poets and the useless little toys of words they make; it may even be another poem about his rejection of the priesthood; it may be an allegory of drug addiction, and the sexual and social withdrawal that often accompanies it (certainly those tweezers, flames and dark gold flashes sound a little like someone cooking up). Either way, the poet expresses a great sadness for these lonely souls – but admiration, too, for their saintly sacrifice, for the purity and discipline of their enterprise, whoever they are.

Where is it written that I must end here,

    incipit, a great gold foliate Q surrounding my
garden wherein nuns fiddle, philosophers discourse on
the augmented fourth, the $\sqrt{-1}$? A window opens, a wax
cylinder crackles, and the castrato's trill is borne on the
wind to the skating peasantry. Across the frozen lake
two boys set fire to a cat; here, the first of thirteen bears
in the Queen's bear garden, its eyes scooped out, its nose
blown full of pepper, shakes two mastiffs from its back and
bellows; the youngest barn burner to be hanged is eight.
His parents are made to watch. Here, beyond the scaffold
and the smoke, a distant hill. On the hill a windmill; in
its engine room a desk; on the desk a psalter; scrawled in
its margin a prayer in the shape of a conch; in that prayer
a devil-snare wound in a spiral of words. I would be the
demon seduced by the riddle, lost in the middle, who
cannot read back.

Ciphers

This is a 'self-descriptive poem', written for a very specific purpose: to trap a demon. These things were really composed: the devil-trap often took the form of a spell or prayer – or, in the seventeenth-century grimoire *The Lesser Key of Solomon*, the device of a pentacle or heptagram.* Here, it takes the form of a coded spiral text, perhaps written in the margin of a medieval manuscript. The idea is that any demon curious enough to read the first line would soon be lost in its coils and unable to find his way back out.

It begins with a paradox: 'Where is it written that I must end here, / incipit . . . ?' *Incipit* means 'here beginneth . . .' and was used by medieval scribes to denote the beginning of a new text or passage; it then came to mean the opening words themselves. *Why* are we to end here, right at the beginning? Indeed, where is it written? It might have been better if we *had* stopped here, as we'll see. This poem has been carefully designed to be, in several senses, a total nightmare.

The *great gold foliate* Q sounds like a majuscule letter at the incipit of an illuminated manuscript. 'Q' for 'question' and Queen, we can assume; but more crucially, Q is also a famous cipher in cryptography. 'Q' uses a constant based on the golden ratio to generate what cryptographers call 'nothing up my sleeve numbers', its initial, above-suspicion numerical

---

* Donaghy had a strong if sceptical interest in theosophy and the occult. I had intended to tackle a late, longish poem of his here, called 'Grimoire'. In the end I found it too screwed up and dark even for me, and I refuse to spend any more time with it than I have to.

values – which, as bizarre as it sounds, is exactly what this poem does too.

So we begin with our big opening question, the shape of our own foolish intrigue, drawn around a curious garden. Whose perversity, initially, seems mild enough; fiddling nuns and debating philosophers hardly smack of Hieronymus Bosch. The philosophers are debating music and mathematics, both of which are woven through the poem. However if we listen to their conversation, they are holding forth on the demonic and the senseless: the *augmented fourth* is the dissonant 'devil's interval' that halves an octave, and lies between B and F in the C scale, the *diabolicus in musica* strongly disapproved of – or at least judiciously avoided – in early church music.

The square root of minus one is an impossible number. (Lacan famously claimed it was the mathematical analogue of the erect male member, an observation which helped no one very much, though Alan Sokal's unpacking of it in *Impostures Intellectuelles* is pretty hilarious.) Here it's a kind of sick doubling of the integer 1, something the poem must do to kick off the Fibonacci series, which in turn generates the golden ratio, the 'Q' cipher on which the poem is based.*

The scene feels medieval, but we hear the otherworldly, unnatural sound of the castrato sing out through an open

---

* There may be a great deal more mathematical intrigue embedded in this poem. There are various ways of arriving at the word-count, but expanding $\sqrt{-1}$ [to 'the square root of minus one' gives either 174 or 175 depending (significantly) on how you count the word 'devil-snare'; 175 is the magic constant of the magic square $n = 7$, and I would say that Donaghy being Donaghy, the chances of this being accidental are about 50/50.

window; we can assume this is Alessandro Moreschi, the only castrato to come near any kind of recording device, although this moves the scene to the turn of the twentieth century. The wrongness of both his voice and this anachronism heralds a descent into hell. The *skating peasantry* foxed me for a while, but I think it's meant to put us in mind of Breughel's 'Winter Landscape with Skaters and a Bird Trap'. This is a strange work, where the presence of the trap so dominates the picture it seems inevitably allegorical: perhaps it represents the inevitability of death, of fate, of capture, even amidst the pleasures of the everyday.

We are then shown three horrors of increasing intensity: the burning cat, the tortured bear, the hanged child. Then we relocate to a distant hill, and we're given a list of precisely five directions (constructed in the creepy, this-is-the-house-that-jack-built rhetorical scheme called 'gradatio', which repeats the end at the next beginning, and creates a linked chain of phrases); these narrow us down to the very spiral of words that is the poem itself.

To return to music and mathematics: the division of 8:13 divides the complete octave 'tonally', at the fifth, the dominant; the augmented fourth divides it evenly, and uncomfortably. As I've mentioned, the numbers the poem is built upon – one, two (mastiffs), three, five and eight (the young barn-burner) and thirteen (bears) – are based on the Fibonacci series, from whose proportions emerge the golden ratio which determines the optimal energy- and space-saving arrangements of many natural phenomena, from the arrangement of sunflower seeds and the dimensions of the DNA molecule to . . . the spiral *shape of a conch*. Into which we have been introduced, and from which there is no way out.

And if we do try to 'read back', where do we find ourselves? *Where is it written that I must end here, / incipit*. In the beginning was our end was our beginning ... And after the first few words, as we can see now – we were *already* lost. How long have we been going round here? Is there more to discover? I suspect so, but will it help us read our way out, or just embed us in its intrigue more deeply? And what does it say about who or what *we* are that we've been locked in here so long, like a bird in a bird-trap especially designed for it?

City of God

When he failed the seminary he came back home
to the Bronx and sat in a back pew
of St Mary's every night reciting the Mass
from memory – quietly, continually –
into his deranged overcoat.
He knew the local phone book off by heart.
He had a system, he'd explain,
perfected by Dominicans in the Renaissance.

To every notion they assigned a saint,
to every saint an altar in a transept of the church.
Glancing up, column by column, altar by altar,
they could remember any prayer they chose.
He'd used it for exams, but the room went wrong –
a strip-lit box exploding slowly as he fainted.
They found his closet papered floor to ceiling
with razored passages from St Augustine.

He needed a perfect cathedral in his head,
he'd whisper, so that by careful scrutiny
the mind inside the cathedral inside the mind
could find the secret order of the world
and remember every drop on every face
in every summer thunderstorm.
And that, he'd insist, looking beyond you,
is why he came home.

I walked him back one evening as the snow
hushed the precincts of his vast invisible temple.
Here was Bruno Street where Bernadette
collapsed, bleeding through her skirt
and died, he had heard, in a state of mortal sin;
here, the site of the bakery fire where Peter stood
screaming on the red-hot fire escape,
his bare feet blistering before he jumped;

and here the storefront voodoo church beneath the el
where the Cuban *bruja* bought black candles,
its window strange with plaster saints and seashells.

Madness

The mnemonic system known as *ars memorae* or 'the method of loci' is a way of 'spatializing' memory by linking information to an imagined physical location. The basic idea is very simple. Visualize the empty interior of a palace, a castle, theatre, cathedral or mall, then mentally place objects within it at significant spots, in a fixed series that can be walked round in sequence. It works a treat, and the system can be used to memorize vast lists, long speeches, and anything else you care to name. The trick of the 'memory palace' became well-known through Cicero and Quintilian, and thereafter popular with everyone from Thomas Aquinas to Hannibal Lecter. Its origins are obscure, though the Greek poet and epigrammatist Simonides is sometimes credited as its inventor. Simonides also came up with the (frankly great) idea of the paid commission, and a ripping yarn is told which neatly consolidates these two strands in his career; it involves unpaid fees, offended gods, collapsed palaces — and recalling the precise location and identity of mangled corpses.*

---

* Donaghy will have learned about all this from Frances Yates's *The Art of Memory*. Ian Duhig informs me that *ars memorae* has a further link to Catholicism through missionaries like Matteo Ricci, who used the idea to impress the Chinese; they borrowed the technique to help students study for their imperial exams. A stranger and rather misguided use of the method of loci appears in the foreword to Ted Hughes's fine anthology *101 Poems to Learn by Heart*, where — having fallen under the dubious spell of mind-map guru Tony Buzan — Hughes suggests narratizing a series of images as a mnemonic aid to remembering the poem itself. This somehow forgets that all a poem *is*

Alas, like all mental systems, it can derange. Look up Charles Hinton and his 4-D cubes as a fine example of what happens when you cram something in the human brain that really doesn't want to go. (Hinton not only invented the tesseract – the net of a 4-D hypercube – but the gunpowder-powered baseball pitching machine, whose early prototypes caused terrible injuries; the guy was trouble.) The lost soul described here already had a broken mind, and was only made worse by his adopting this literally maddening system. *His deranged overcoat* is a wonderful example of the transferred epithet (it's basically a telegraphed version of 'the overcoat of the deranged man', which produces something that is both a metaphor and a metonym).

The memory man, like Borges's *Funes the Memorious*, seems good for little else but his all-consuming shtick. His seminary exam fell apart when the mental space where he'd kept his memoranda did the same. If the space won't keep its shape, if the palace falls . . . the system is useless. But instead of abandoning his system, the poor man decides to reinforce it, and then decides that the secret key to everything is in *the mind inside the cathedral inside the mind*. But his error isn't in internalizing the mnemonic system, but in projecting it outwardly. He superimposes his whole theology over the South Bronx, making a *City of God* very different from that of

---

is a mnemonic aid made of words, whose primary aim is to get itself memorized – through original speech, concise phrasing, rhythmic force and lyric weave. I once saw Donaghy sustain a half-hour conversation with Hughes on his *Shakespeare and the Goddess of Complete Being*. He was too embarrassed to admit he hadn't read a word of it. Which does suggest that if you can bluff like *that*, you probably don't have to remember anything.

Saint Augustine's vision. It wasn't just his exams that went to hell – what he creates is what Augustine feared most: his title in full is *De Civitate Dei contra Paganos*. His faith was shaken to the core, and what threatened it has become physically manifest. The city he now beholds has fallen to those pagans, and how horribly.

Listen to the sibilant stillness of *hushed the precincts of his vast invisible temple*, and its invoking of Donaghy's white-noisy 'beyond'. 'Precinct' also means 'enclosure' (L. *cingere*, 'to gird', is cognate with everything from *zone* to *enceinte*). Our failed priest has made the local space a mad, closed zone he can more or less control. But if the evening has a sepulchral calm, what he has mapped onto it is nightmarish. In his madness he has confused not only space, but time and person; the lives of the saints are confused with his neighbours. This would be bad enough, but the vision has been infected . . . And the saints now fall into his own personal hell. According to Google maps, there is no 'Bruno Street' in the Bronx. The allusion here is to the Dominican polymath and heretic Giordano Bruno, who died by *auto-da-fé* in 1600.* St Bernadette – Marie Bernarde Soubirous, whose Marian vision made her famous as the 'Lady of Lourdes' – is here presented as a 'fallen woman', dying in sin. St Peter's feet let him down a lot: when

---

* Bruno was also a champion of *ars memorae*. Donaghy had began a PhD on Bruno, and had attempted to complete it in a single year, aided by the appropriate pharmaceuticals and a specially fitted-out chair, which didn't require him to do anything but hit the books all day and most of the night. He ended up reading his own dreams in the form of scrolling text, and soon had lost the plot completely. He once showed me a textbook from that year; he'd taken a highlighter pen to every single line in the *entire book*.

he tried to walk on water, his faith wavered, and he was also queasy about allowing Jesus to wash his feet at the Last Supper. The bakery fire here also echoes the Great Fire of Rome, which Nero sought to blame on the Christians, and for which Peter was crucified (after the *quo vadis* business). Here, though, Peter is not martyred and raised to heaven, but pitched into the flames.

Finally, what are we to make of this last little horror? A church gone wrong, beneath the elevated railway, where the Cuban witches (a *bruja* is a sorceress) would stock up on black candles for their black masses. Given that this place probably *was* real, what did our friend see other than the physical confirmation of his own vision? A fallen city where his beloved saints are mass-produced and miniaturized, nothing more than cheap talismans to be recruited for the forces of evil? We find the confirmation of our worst fears exactly where we look for them, but especially when we look this hard.

The Classics

I remember it like it was last night,
Chicago, the back room of Flanagan's
malignant with accordions and cigarettes,
Joe Cooley bent above his Paolo Soprani,
its asthmatic bellows pumping as if to revive
the half-corpse strapped about it.
It's five a.m. Everyone's packed up.
His brother Seamus grabs Joe's elbow mid-arpeggio.
'Wake up, man. We have to catch a train.'
His eyelids fluttering, opening. The astonishment . . .

I saw this happen. Or heard it told so well
I've staged the whole drunk memory:
What does it matter now? It's ancient history.
Who can name them? Where lie their bones and armour?

Myth

The role of the accordionist in classical myth cannot be understated. The large 'piano' version of the instrument – as opposed to the lovely little *bosca*, the button box melodeon or concertina – is often loathed in traditional Irish music sessions because it's so overwhelmingly loud: I've seen signs on bar doors consisting of a piano accordion in a circle with a red line through it. Although it doesn't have as bad a reputation as the bodhrán, the goatskin frame drum that was Donaghy's main instrument. When asked the best way to play it, the great uillean piper Seamus Ennis famously answered, 'with a penknife'. (Or someone famously did; the remark has multiple provenances.) The bodhrán has this notoriety because too many confuse owning one with being able to play one. Michael liked to recall the occasion when he saw Frankie Gavin, the legendary fiddle virtuoso, halt a session mid-tune to snatch the stick from a goat-spanker's hand and yell, 'You're spoiling it for everyone!' Michael, however, played his with great skill. His drum was made not from goat but ass-skin, and probably chosen only because it was replete with comic potential. And a good box player is as fine a thing as you'll hear, as Michael often conceded.

But that was a classic, that one; remember the time Joe Cooley fell asleep while *still playing*? The muscle-memory of the traditional Irish musician is so strong that even sleep can't affect it; that in itself says something about the long roots of the tradition, which seem to reach down into the individual unconscious. Musicians often say that after a few years 'the instrument plays you'. What's not always appreciated is that this is *almost* literally the case – or at least it's a decidedly non-metaphorical experience: through years of repetitive practice, a perfect simulacrum of the real instrument now exists in your brain, and does its own thing. (Although I suspect such experiences are common enough in anyone who has learned a similarly repetitive task, speaking as one who has occasionally woken up mid-lecture, by which I mean the lecture I was giving at the time.) One can simply disappear, or, as here, fall asleep: the accordion even takes over as a life-support machine, an external lung.

This time, our speaker genuinely wants to be believed: Joe Cooley – unlike 'Patrolman Jack O'Ryan' of 'The Hunter's Purse' – was very real, and a legendary master of the button accordion. (Even his red Paolo Soprani has mythical status, and its current whereabouts are hotly debated.) Anyway: it's a classic, a hero's tale. Who cares if it was true? Whether I was there or not, I might as well have been. In the final two lines Donaghy suddenly switches to a classical register, to immensely moving effect. As Patrick Kavanagh said in 'Epic', *'Homer made the Iliad out of such a local row'*; Donaghy's point, too, is that it's in such 'low' materials that our heroes are found and our epics founded. But what does it matter to us, really? These heroes are as dead to us as Achilles, Hector or the nameless fallen at Troy. Yet we still tell their stories, compulsively.

This is a free-ish unrhymed sonnet, each line having roughly four or five strong stresses. However, there's a lovely metrical feature here whose effect is instinctively felt, but whose mechanism is quite complex, though I'll try to sketch it out simply. It concerns another level of prosodic subtlety that sits on top of the poetic metre that shapes the line. *I remember it like it was last night* is close to what we call a 'phraseme', or a near-cliché. These stock phrases get filed in our brain as 'words' rather than sentences, which is to say they don't need to be processed along the rule of syntax: we already *know* what they mean, and just like single words, they can be swapped for synonyms. This phrase would be filed under 'indelible memory stuff', just the way we file 'like the back of my hand' under 'thorough knowledge'. We file these along the 'axis of selection', where we both store our individual words and connect them through their shared qualities. Now: as soon as something *becomes* a word, or is 'lexicalized' – it takes only one principal stress, much in the way a mug needs only one handle. As a result, the natural prosody of the sentence *I remember it like it was last night* – x x/x x / x x / / – might be delivered more as x x x x x x x x x /' – leaving only *one* intonationally distinguished accent on 'night'. But when the poet says *What does it matter now? It's ancient history. / Who can name them? Where lie their bones and armour?* things are very different. The throwaway cliché 'I remember it like it was last night' *should* be thrown away for the poem to really work – otherwise it can't manage the symbolic contrast between the first line's anecdotal chattiness, and the final lines' beautiful 'classicizing' of the anecdote. We might even scan *Who can name them? Where lie their bones and armour?* as /x //? // x / x /x? – leaving us with a line that feels like it might have *seven* strong stresses, in contrast to just one in the first line. A great poet like Donaghy will often use cliché and collocation for both metrical and rhetorical contrast. One still occasionally hears that 'in a poem, each word should receive its due weight', but next time you do, ignore it.

(A postscript: I was writing on this poem when I noticed something off about the font, which wasn't my usual Book Antiqua. On closer inspection it turned out to be Palatino, Michael's own favourite. This typographical relic originated from a Word doc he'd sent me many years ago; the font had survived fourteen years of cutting and pasting, which gave me a bit of a sad start.)

A Disaster

We were ships in the night.
We thought her rockets were fireworks.

Our radio was out, and we didn't know
The band was only playing to calm the passengers.

Christ, she was lovely all lit up,
Like a little diamond necklace!

Try to understand. Out here in the dark
We thought we were missing the time of our lives.

We could almost smell her perfume.
And she went down in sight of us.

The conceit

This disarmingly simple little ten-liner exploits the old convention of feminizing ships. The poem it superficially resembles is Stevie Smith's 'Not Waving but Drowning': *It must have been too cold for him his heart gave way, / They said. / Oh, no no no, it was too cold always / (Still the dead one lay moaning) / I was much too far out all my life / And not waving but drowning*. The poem is clearly not about a boat; it's an 'extended conceit', a longer metaphorical comparison. Since the poet doesn't actually mention the real subject, I suppose we could call this poem an allegory. However, one possible theme is given clearly enough: you can read it as being about a woman, and she's a disaster. We might initially assume the poem was just about the *Titanic* – *The band was only playing to calm the passengers* is a cliché of the *Titanic* story – and that the speaker is describing the SS *Californian*'s notorious indifference to the plight of the sinking ship. Distress flares were ignored, wireless operators failed to transmit warnings, and Captain Stanley Lord was too intent on looking after his own vessel when the drowning passengers could still have been saved after the boat had gone down.

However, *We were ships in the night* should alert us immediately to the conceit, since it stagily invokes the old cliché for a chance romantic encounter, 'to pass like ships in the night'. But the word 'pass' is conspicuous by its absence here. The speaker doesn't have the consoling comfort of knowing he *was* bound in another direction, and therefore unable to help. He was all *too* able. So what could we have done? Yes, we might have sailed the same waters, but the distance and the dark afforded us some convenient misreadings. *Christ, she was lovely all lit up / Like a little diamond necklace!* Our own warped self-interest didn't help either: we even *resented* this pleasure cruiser. Hell, we were missing out on all the fun. But our excuses are already being rehearsed. *Our radio was out* we might read as 'we were too thoughtlessly self-absorbed to contact her'. But the fireworks we saw turned out to be distress flares, the fairy lights were flames, and the music we heard was being played to calm the panicked. A disaster, all right . . . But if we're honest, one as much of our own negligent making as her own.*

For me, the killer line is *We could almost smell her perfume*. The speaker is now too upset to be bothered to sustain the distancing comfort of his own metaphor, and gives up on it entirely. This means that the line which follows, 'she went down in sight of us', has now escaped the conceit, and can be read literally. Our friend went down – right there on the street, in the club, in some hopeless hell of a suburban afternoon, and we did nothing. But we had no perspective. Try to understand; put yourself in our position.

---

* Greta Stoddart has pointed out to me that the poem can be read straightforwardly as one about the kind of 'survivors' guilt' that can follow any proximate disaster, and the things we do to exonerate ourselves; there's no need to invoke any woman as its subject. This reading is as plausible as my own, but I suspect Donaghy knew what he was doing. Simple, symbolic poems of this kind often allow us a greater variety of interpretations – with the result that our readings often end up telling us far more about ourselves than they do about the poem or the poet. (Frost's 'The Road Not Taken' is a classic example.)

'Smith'

What is this fear before the unctuous teller?
Why does it seem to take a forger's nerve
To make my signature come naturally?
Naturally? But every signature's
A trick we learn to do, consistently,
Like Queequeg's cross, or Whistler's butterfly.
Perhaps some childhood spectre grips my hand
Every time I'm asked to sign my name.

Maybe it's Sister Bridget Agatha
Who drilled her class in Christ and penmanship
And sneered *affected* at my seven-year-old scrawl.
True, it was unreadably ornate
And only one of five that I'd developed,
But try as I might I couldn't recall
The signature that I'd been born with.

Later, in my teens, I brought a girl,
My first, to see the Rodin exhibition.
I must have ranted on before each bronze;
Metal of blood and honey . . . Pure Sir Kenneth Clark.
And those were indeed the feelings I wanted to have,
But I could tell that she was unimpressed.
She fetched our coats. I signed the visitor's book,
My name embarrassed back into mere words.

No, I'm sure it all began years later.
I was twenty, and the girl was even younger.
We chose the hottest August night on record
And a hotel with no air-conditioning.
We tried to look adult. She wore her heels
And leant against the cigarette machine as,
Arching an eyebrow, I added to the register
The name I'd practised into spontaneity –
Surely it wasn't – *Mr and Mrs Smith*?

It's all so long ago and lost to me,
And yet, how odd, I remember a moment so pure,
In every infinite detail indelible,
When I gripped her small shoulders in my hands,
Steadying her in her slippery ride,
And I looked up into her half-closed eyes . . .
Dear friend, whatever is most true in me
Lives now and for ever in that instant,
The night I forged a hand, not mine, not anyone's,
And in that tiny furnace of a room,
Forged a thing unalterable as iron.

Lies

It's a fine day in your poetic apprenticeship when you wake up and realize you can lie about absolutely everything. An artist's allegiance is to the truth, not the facts, and facts are often the things you have to change to make the poem more truthful. Like so many of Donaghy's poems, much rests on the title, but we'll get to that. This is a great, apparently weightless disquisition on personae – who *is* it, exactly, that we present to the world and to each other? Our signature, our legal marks, are not like our fingerprints; they're not something we're born with. We're required to invent a device by which we can validate ourselves; and thereafter, by bizarre human convention, all it takes to generate our own authenticating watermark of personality and neurosis and credit-card debt is a pen and paper. If we want to be taken for *one* person – we could easily sustain two, three or many more, but that makes the authorities uncomfortable – we need to perfect just one signature. Being or pretending to be just one person is a trick; most of us host a whole bunch of folk.

After one of the most brilliantly memorable first lines in the English language – try signing something before the bank clerk again, and *not* thinking *What is this fear before the unctuous teller?** – the poet considers some touchstone examples.

---

* It succeeds for a number of reasons, but partly because the succession of vowels [aw / ee / oh / uh / eh] has a lovely, varied, roughly forward progression, and the first plosive stop doesn't occur until the final content word. So until the creepy *teller* we get a whisper, a hiss. Until that point, all is either under-the-radar function (these words usually take little stress, because they don't have to be consciously

The 'savage' Queequeg is the chief harpooner of the *Pequod* in *Moby Dick*, and his unlettered signature was a cross;* by deliberate contrast, the poet then adduces the ultra-refined painter J. A. M. Whistler, who turned the JW of his initials into a rather affected little butterfly monogram. But the speaker has neither's confidence. Where does his uncertainty come from? Guilt-ridden Catholic childhood, most likely, and the nuns he was terrified by in school. Even then, the whole exercise was ruined by self-consciousness: how the hell can you get your own signature *right*? In the third stanza the scene is one of clumsy cultural aspiration, another Donaghy theme. (As they say, you don't have to be Sigmund Freud to guess that it's Donaghy's father who keeps stumbling behind him.) The speaker badly overreaches himself, failing to convince either himself or his date of his aesthetic sensitivity and expertise. No: if something has to be forged – it has to be truer than this.

It's all so long ago and lost to me, yet the poet claims he can recall their lovemaking with eidetic clarity. *How odd*. Just so; but in the double sense of the word *forge* and its related pun *Smith* lie a kind of solution. The room the young lovers take is as deathly hot as a smithy's forge. They use the name *Smith*

---

processed) or light fricative and liquid sounds around this big rolling vowel, coming towards you like your doom.

* It was only a *cross* because the printer couldn't replicate the 'queer round figure' in Melville's original manuscript. 'But at this question, Queequeg, who had twice or thrice before taken part in similar ceremonies, looked no ways abashed; but taking the offered pen, copied upon the paper, in the proper place, an exact counterpart of a queer round figure which was tattooed upon his arm; so that through Captain Peleg's obstinate mistake touching his appellative, it stood something like this: . . .'

to sign in; 'Smith' is almost the *eponymous* anonym – one so clichéd, the poet can't quite believe his own lack of imagination. But that initial forgery allows them entrance to a place where they can now forge something authentic, struck new from the malleable yet iron-like substance of their own love. What was forged was neither the mask of a persona nor a self, but a deep connection. This poet believes that who we are to one another is far more important than who we are to ourselves.

Buried within the poem are a few classic moments of Donaghy instability, the sort of thing that he would weave in so seamlessly and lightly it could take years to notice. Firstly, who is the *Dear friend*? Do they just authenticate the sincerity of his address, or is there something more to it? Secondly, look at the line *No, I'm sure it all began years later*. This answers the question *Why does it seem to take a forger's nerve / To make my signature come naturally?* Despite affording him an experience that sounds, to me at least, overwhelmingly positive, the forging of *Smith* at the hotel reception-desk was also the origin of the poet's adult fear. Go figure. Thirdly, we must consider whether or not the poet is hinting that he has used his 'forger's nerve' and our own sentimentality to blind us to the fact that the whole thing is – whisper it – completely made up.

(This was the first poem of Michael's I ever read. I was at a very insecure stage of my own apprenticeship, and I had just discovered, to my immense relief, that most contemporary poetry was pretty bad and could be swiftly dismissed. I recall reading this poem in *Poetry Review* next to a photograph of a depressingly handsome young man, and realizing to my further dismay that it might actually be good. Then I read it again, and took a much simpler delight in it being plainly wonderful. *This* was why I was in this game. I met Donaghy shortly after, and in that younger and greener incarnation asked him if the story of 'Smith' was true. 'For Chrissake – of course it wasn't!' he answered, somehow managing a tone that was simultaneously withering and kind. I still think it *was*.)

Erratum

I touch the cold flesh of a god in the V and A,
the guard asleep in his chair, and I'm shocked
to find it's plaster. These are the reproduction rooms,
where the David stands side by side with the Moses
and Trajan's column (in two halves).
It reminds me of the inventory sequence in *Citizen Kane*.
It reminds me of an evening twenty years ago.

And all at once I'm there, at her side,
turning the pages as she plays
from the yellowed song sheets I rescued from a bookstall:
Dodd's setting of *Antony and Cleopatra*. All very improving.
'Give me my robe and crown,' she warbles
in a Victorian coloratura. 'I have immoral longings in me.'

I want to correct her – the word on the page is
immortal – but I'm fourteen and scandalized.
(I knew there were no innocent mistakes.
I'd finished *Modern Masters: Freud*
before she snatched and burned it. 'Filth' –
yanking each signature free of the spine,
'Filth. Filth. Filth.')

The song is over. But when she smiles at me,
I'm on the verge of tears, staring down at the gap-
toothed grimace of our old Bechstein. 'What's wrong?'
What's *wrong*? I check the word again. She's right. Immoral.
She shows me the printer's slip, infecting
the back page of every copy, like,
she might have said, the first sin.

The guard snorts in his dream. I take my palm away
still cool from what I'd taken to be marble.
And when I get that moment back, it's later;
I'm sobbing on her shoulder and I can't say why.
So she suggests another visit to the furnace, where,
to comfort me, perhaps, we rake the cinders with the music
till they chink and spark, and shove the pages
straight to the white core to watch them darken as if ageing,
blacken, enfold, like a sped-up film of blossoms in reverse.

Fakes

Now *here's* a tale. It's a convoluted one, so bear with me; this twisted, twisting story is worth our careful attention. The three interwoven scenarios described are in themselves fairly straightforward. One is real – the plaster reproduction rooms in the Victoria and Albert Museum, which Donaghy frequently haunted; one is imaginary, a scene from Orson Welles's classic, *Citizen Kane*; and one is false or faked – a memory the poet claims of listening to his mother sing at her Bechstein. (Not that it matters, but Donaghy's mother didn't play the piano.) Donaghy's love of the nested or self-similar image is allowed to run riot here. The opening scene seems dreamlike, though the location is quite genuine. Anyone who has stood between those two immense lumps of Trajan's column will testify to the reproduction room's eerie surrealism; it looks like a scrapyard has just bought the entire contents of Western culture as a job lot.

What jolts the speaker is the surprise of finding that the sculpture of a god is not chiselled from marble, but is instead a plaster copy cast from the original. (Here, the god, the marble god and the plaster god may stand in deliberate analogy to the real room, the imaginary film and the false memory.) *The inventory sequence in Citizen Kane* refers to the scene where Charles Foster Kane's infinite, impossibly miscellaneous belongings are auctioned off at Xanadu – which does indeed put you in mind of the organized chaos of the V&A's reproduction room. The poet also wants us to remember that immediately after the inventory scene, we see the symbol of Kane's uncorrupted youth, his sled 'Rosebud' – which explains the mystery of his final word – thrown into a furnace. (We merely need to keep this in mind for now.) This false god also takes the poet back to what is probably a lie or a false memory. Like the plaster god, this deals with the cheaply flawed reproduction of an original: a musical setting of *Antony and Cleopatra*.

I doubt this setting exists. The only one I know about is Samuel Barber's, from 1966; these yellowed song-sheets are from another era. The Revd William Dodd compiled a popular book called *The Beauties of William Shakespeare*, and he may have provided the composer's name: Dodd is rather more famous as a forger, who was hanged at Tyburn gallows in 1777. I doubt that the poet recalls a real occasion either: Donaghy was born in 1954, which places this episode in 1968 (*I'm fourteen and scandalized*); however, the poem was composed about 1991, meaning the poet was around thirty-eight at the time. *Errata*, in which this poem appeared, was published in 1993. I mention all this only to show that the poet is writing using a persona, and, as a little private joke with himself, claiming to be exactly thirty-four (most probably because thirty-four – yes, here we go again – is a Fibonacci number).

The woman makes what the young boy thinks is a 'Freudian slip', and he's mortified. (I assume it's the speaker's mother, though I suppose it could be an aunt, older sister, or music teacher.) She sings *I have immoral longings* . . . But the word on the score is *immortal*. Shakespeare's Cleopatra does indeed say 'immortal longings', just before she takes her own life with the asp: *Give me my robe. Put on my crown. I have / Immortal longings in me. Now no more / The juice of Egypt's grape shall moist this lip*. But no, the mother is quite right: Dodd's intention really was *immoral*, and he went to the trouble of printing up an erratum slip (the echo of 'Freudian slip' is deliberate) which was inserted into the score. It infects 'like the first sin' because the 'wrong' correction *itself* is an error that has infected everything. A typo is one thing; but a mistake which is deliberately inserted into every correct text is an abomination. *Every* reproduction of this Cleopatra has fallen, and is a cheap, shoddy and fatally imperfect replica. And this transgressive, sexual urge is placed in the mouth of the mother – a woman of immaculate reputation, who considers Freud *filth*, and believes in original sin. The boy is understandably shocked.

The reverie or memory ends; the poet withdraws his cold hand from the worthless plaster statue. He then remembers something else. In an effort to pacify him, his mother/teacher burned the entire score, as she had earlier his *Modern Masters: Freud*. (This mother/Cleopatra is a grand one for the book-burning. In Act 5 of *Antony and Cleopatra*, Cleopatra says *I am fire and air; my other elements / I give to baser life*.) They watch the pages burn in the furnace *like a sped-up film of blossoms in reverse* – just what burning pages can look like, as they pack themselves back into black buds . . . Innocent, as yet unsullied by their own mature flowering: this is also very much a poem about pubescent rites of passage and self-disgust. Those black blossoms might now bring to mind the burning 'Rosebud', the symbol of Kane's innocent joy (which also appears to 'burn backwards' in Welles's film). This, we can be certain, is what the author has also lost here. He now knows we are *all* God's mistakes, his shoddy, dirty, infected replicas.

The Tuning

If anyone asks you how I died, say this:
The angel of death came in the form of a moth
And landed on the lute I was repairing.
I closed up shop
And left the village on the quietest night of summer,
The summer of my thirtieth year,
And went with her up through the thorn forest.

Tell them I heard yarrow stalks snapping beneath my feet
And heard a dog bark far off, far off.
That's all I saw or heard,
Apart from the angel at ankle level leading me,
Until we got above the treeline and I turned
To look for the last time on the lights of home.

That's when she started singing.
It's written that the voice of the god of Israel
Was the voice of many waters.
But this was the sound of trees growing,
The noise of a pond thrown into a stone.

When I turned from the lights below to watch her sing,
I found the angel changed from moth to woman,
Singing inhuman intervals through her human throat,
The notes at impossible angles justified.

If you understand, friend, explain to them
So they pray for me. How could I go back?
How could I bear to hear the heart's old triads —
Clatter of hooves, the closed gate clanging,
A match scratched toward a pipe —
How could I bear to hear my children cry?

I found a rock that had the kind of heft
We weigh the world against
And brought it down fast against my forehead
Again, again, until blood drenched my chest
And I was safe and real forever.

Prophecies

This early poem of Donaghy's takes the form of a myth. (It's *alarmingly* early; I'll explain the reason for my alarm shortly.) The poem answers an unanswerable: what is the nature of the world that exists beyond our limited human perception, and what happens if we're exposed to it? The story is simple, strange, and beautifully told. A luthier – one who specializes, if you like, in *the heart's old triads*, an expert in the mechanics of human music – is visited by an angel. It is named as the angel of death, so we know the outcome of the story in the second line; it will be the manner, not the fact of the speaker's death that will surprise us. She comes in the form of a tiny moth, and she leads the speaker, mid-summer and mid-life, to a place high above the village and away from the human, the local, the reassuringly known. Her purpose, as they used to say, is to 'lay a trip' on him – but the reason for her choice of victim is not explained, beyond the possible hubris of his profession. What she decides to vouchsafe is something that would normally be quite beyond the scope of human hearing. He then hears intolerable, infrasonic, or logically impossible sounds: *trees growing, a pond thrown into a stone*. We know from our myths that news from the non-human realm is usually dangerous, and tends to carry dire consequences for the listener.

And then she sings. She sings in a human voice, but sings no human music, with *the notes at impossible angles justified*. 'Justified' echoes 'just intonation', but here means 'to make fit or to arrange precisely', to adjust to the exact shape, size, or position – i.e. just the way a maker of musical instruments might understand the word. And at the touch of this terrible, divine music, *all* human sound is ruined for him. He can no longer bear its racket, its pain, its wretched sentimental simplicity. The only option is to fully enter the new reality he's been shown, through the only way he can: the act of suicide. This renders him *real*. Our condition of becoming and of passing makes us more ghosts than real things; so the end of ghosthood is the beginning of reality.

But *safe*? *Safe* may seem an odd word here, but it's a key term for Donaghy, and far closer to the word 'dead' in his mind than in ours. (For this reason, death probably presented him with a happier prospect.) For Donaghy, 'alive' implied a zone of pain and of constant threat. We called his posthumous collection *Safest*, because that was the name of the folder in which he'd stored his final drafts – the less-ready work was filed under *safe* or *safer* – and it also drew attention to the finest poem in that book, 'The Safe House'. We might then have recalled this poem too, with its distressing and prophetic intimations of mortality. That the poem was such an early one is particularly unnerving; it was a survivor from *Slivers*, his first collection, later disowned as part-juvenilia. But as Antonio Porchia once wrote: *Before I travelled my road I was my road*. Sometimes it seems Michael Donaghy was one of those souls who arrive here already knowing their entire story, even if he preferred to put it to the back of his mind. For that reason, I tend to think of him as being not so much 'dead' as 'finished'.

The Excuse

Please hang up. I try again.
'My father's sudden death has shocked us all'
Even me, and I've just made it up,
Like the puncture, the cheque in the post,
Or my realistic cough. As I'm believed,
I'm off the hook. But something snags and holds.

My people were magicians. Home from school,
I followed a wire beneath the table to
A doorbell. I rang it. My father looked up.

Son, when your uncle gets me on the phone
He won't let go. I had to rig up something.

Midnight. I pick up and there's no one there,
No one, invoked, beyond that drone. But if
I had to rig up something, and I do,
Let my excuse be this, and this is true:
I fear for him and grieve him more than any,
This most deceiving and deceived of men . . .
Please hang up and try again.

Strange loops

Like many people, Donaghy had a difficult relationship with the truth; and like many poets, this was often born of incompetent necessity. (His standard excuse for double-bookings and last-minute, just-can't-face-it bail-outs was 'My uncle has been taken ill in Milton Keynes'.)

The poem opens with the poet apparently trying to lie to cover his own professional absence, using the perhaps over-ambitious excuse that his father has died. *Please hang up* – the recorded instruction that greets a misdialled number in the UK – means he has either waited too long to dial, or dialled the wrong number. The phrase abbreviates a longer message: 'The number you have dialled has not been recognized. Please hang up and try again.' *As I'm believed, / I'm off the hook* refers not to *this* tasteless excuse, but to earlier, successful excuses (the sense is *As I'm [always] believed [when I say those things]*). On those occasions, he's *off the hook*. This is a pun: not just 'got away with it', but 'the phone receiver is off the hook, so one can't be contacted'.

The phrase 'My father's sudden death has shocked us all' sounds far more like nervous rehearsal than real speech. Is he bottling out and *deliberately* misdialling, or hesitating to dial at all? He's shocked himself at this new addition to his list of standard excuses, and is suddenly queasy about lumping his dead father in with the puncture, the lost cheque payment, the cough. He's surpassed himself. (The inability to access the feeling you were *supposed* to host on any given occasion would often torment Donaghy, lightly: at his father's wake he really did sit by the corpse and catch himself thinking 'Jesus, if I can't get a poem out of *this*.') The poet is *not* off the fish-hook of his guilty responsibility. His conscience snags him.

The occasion prompts a memory – a standard Donaghy stratagem – which might explain or excuse his behaviour. Lies and excuses run in the family, though they're not executed without love. (*My people were magicians* is a kind of buried epigraph to the entire book *Conjure*, in which this was the first poem. Many other poems refer to it, and develop this theme of magical lineage.) The poet's father has made an excuse-generator: a doorbell he can ring in his own home, so he has a plausible reason to get his windbag brother off the line when he calls. *I followed a wire beneath the table to / A doorbell* is a typically cheeky line-break, enacting the pause and the surprise of what the speaker finds. The key detail to bear in mind here is that his father rings his *own* doorbell: there's no one there. And now the younger poet has rung it too.

The last stanza flash-forwards to the present again. It's later that night; witching hour. I suspect the speaker has picked up because he thinks the phone has rung – he wouldn't be surprised to hear the drone of the dial tone, if he'd merely put the phone to his ear; but there's no one there at the end, no one on the other side. I think what he's hearing is the call he has placed to himself earlier – *I rang it* – and what happens now proceeds from that existential short-circuit. This 'strange loop' is the inverse of the one through which Douglas Hofstadter (whose work Donaghy loved) thinks our own consciousness and selfhood is constituted; that feedback loop creates, but this one negates. *But if / I had to rig up something* isn't an easy line to understand. Rig up for what? To excuse himself from this endless communion with his long-dead father, with himself, or from his endless lie?

By way of compensation for his earlier blasphemy and disrespect, he now makes a formal statement in far more honourable and sincere language, which we are invited to either believe or not. (*This is true* is, by now, the Cretan paradox.) *I fear for him and grieve him more than any, / This most deceiving and deceived of men* . . . That illogical verb – how can one *fear* for the dead? – tells me that Donaghy is doing two things: hosting a fear his father cannot, i.e. 'I will fear on your behalf'; and referring *both* to his father and to himself. (*Conjure* ends with an even more complex poem called 'Haunts', in which the voices of father and son are deliberately interfused.) He has become his father. He is, like him, a magician, a deceiver – and he is self-deceived, which all liars eventually become: duped by their own endless excuses, they wind up barely knowing who they are. *Please hang up and try again.* We know the dead don't pick up. But what does it mean to call up *yourself*, to conjure yourself – then find no one at home?

A Repertoire

'Play us one we've never heard before'
we'd ask this old guy in our neighbourhood.
He'd rosin up a good three or four
seconds, stalling, but he always could.
This was the Bronx in 1971,
when every night the sky was pink with arson.
He ran a bar beneath the el, the Blarney Stone,
and there one Easter day he sat us down
and made us tape as much as he could play;
'I gave you these. Make sure you put that down',
meaning all he didn't have to say.

All that summer we slept on fire escapes,
or tried to sleep, while sirens or the brass
from our neighbour's Tito Puente tapes
kept us up and made us late for Mass.
I found our back door bent back to admit
beneath the thick sweet reek of grass
a nest of needles, bottle caps, and shit.
By August Tom had sold the Blarney Stone
to Puerto Ricans, paid his debts in cash
but left enough to fly his body home.

The bar still rises from the South Bronx ash,
its yellow neon buzzing in the noonday
dark beneath the el, a sheet-steel door
bolted where he played each second Sunday.
'Play me one I've never heard before'
I'd say, and whether he recalled those notes
or made them up, or – since it was Tom who played –
whether it was something in his blood
(cancer, and he was childless and afraid)
I couldn't tell you. And he always would.

The tradition

Play me one I've never heard before. Both traditional music and poetry have their origins in an oral, mnemonic culture. In Donaghy's mind, music has the same conflicted relationship with recording technology as the poem does with the book. Donaghy would always perform *without* a book, entirely from memory, and had a thousand other poems on his tongue beside his own. This poem is about just such mental repositories, and their importance in relation to two other parallel events: the death of an individual and what dies with him, and the death of a community and what dies with it. Tom is putting his temporal affairs in order, and worries he will die before his repertoire of tunes is properly archived and the tape-machine has gleaned his teeming brain; given the cultural importance of what he carries within him, he's right to be meticulous in his instructions.

Donaghy often echoes a physical action in an enjambed line-break. Here, *He'd rosin up a good three or four / seconds, stalling* enacts Tom's hesitation, preparing his bow while he readies himself to deliver his routine miracle. (Later, another mid-phrase break intensifies its own surprise: *its yellow neon buzzing in the noonday / dark beneath the el . . .*) *Easter* is, you will recall, a time associated with dramatic checkouts. There are no accidental details in Donaghy's poems; Thomas was a key figure in Donaghy's iconography, and given Doubting Thomas's role in the Easter story would not be invoked here by accident. It may point to Tom's fictional status, but there's as much chance he was real; we can't know.*

---

* Michael was also attracted by the infinity mirror of his name, *Thomas the Twin* or *Didymus*: Thomas *also* means 'the twin'. (His son's

Either way it's a good time to depart, and Tom's return to Ireland (albeit in a box), his 'exile's end', coincides with the dispersal and death of the Irish community in the Bronx as larger and even poorer Hispanic communities moved in. It's fair to say the speaker doesn't adopt a neutral attitude towards this natural cycle: *the brass / from our neighbour's Tito Puente tapes / kept us up and made us late for Mass* is an annoyance, but no one wants to find *a nest of needles, bottle caps, and shit* at their back door. There's a kind of knowing xenophobia to this – or it *should* be knowing, since the author is well aware that the Irish, too, are merely incomers who have sustained their culture in Manna-hata in no less an artificial way. *The Blarney Stone* beneath the elevated railway can be read as 'absurd romantic Irish signifier in an urban and alien context'.

This 'repertoire' is a vast cultural repository of jigs and reels, hornpipes and polkas, an Irish Library of Babel hosted by Tom's memory. Humans are temporary, communities are temporary, but the repertoire survives. The subject of Irish music is the only time Donaghy gets close to dewy-eyed; another Donaghy poem, 'The Reprieve', addresses a similar subject – the true story of the bizarre quid pro quo regularly worked by Francis O'Neill, the great archivist of Irish traditional music, in the course of his tune-collecting. O'Neill was a police chief in Chicago; on a weekend, there was no shortage of drunken Irish musicians cluttering up the cells – but they

---

middle name is Tomás.) In some Gnostic scriptures, Thomas is the twin of either Judas or Jesus himself: that's a hell of an 'either'. He also features in a genuinely brilliant poem about faith, called 'Reprimands'. I have no idea why I haven't discussed it in this book, but I suspect myself of an act of suppression.

could negotiate their early release in exchange for their repertoires. O'Neill would sit beside them and carefully notate their tunes, while they tried to play them the same way twice. It's a fine poem, but a sentimental one. 'A Repertoire', however, has no trace of mawkishness: it's a moving tribute to the kind of exceptional individual upon whom human culture depends, and a poem about the ends of natural cycles, what we should let go, and what we must preserve.

Irish traditional music is a structurally simple one that nonetheless can be played with devastating virtuosity. Tom was probably carrying the old forms so deep in his circuitry that it was, for him, no great feat to improvise a wholly new tune that sounded as if it had been around for ever. He was absolutely dependable.* And then you realize – how could this tradition have ever come *about*, never mind survive, other than through people like Tom and their brilliant improvisations? Sometimes a new tune that someone will bring to a session will take hold; it's called for the next night, and the night after, and spreads like a happy virus through the community, usually shedding the name of its composer. Either

---

* A few poets, being as well-versed in their own art as Tom was in his, can improvise half-decent poetry if they have to; Wallace Stevens was one such, I gather. However, Donaghy was the only poet I have met who had Coleridge's (alleged) ability to *dream* them. (I don't mean the sort of thing where you wake at 3 a.m. to scribble down the phrase 'the silent dwarves have eaten all the pesto – THIS IS GOLD/IMPORTANT' and fall asleep again.) The only dream-stanza of Michael's that I know made it into print – he insisted that he hadn't changed a word – was the following, from a poem called 'A Miracle': *The angels have come early for the miracle. / They've gotten into the bar and drunk it dry. / Grinning, staggering, shedding feathers, / They can barely stand up, let alone fly.*

way, whether Tom remembered them, made them up, or somehow drew them from the deep well of the tradition (it was *in his blood*, a phrase Donaghy turns to to tell us of the personal urgency of the exercise) is neither here not there. The point is: he always would.

Riddle

I am the book you'll never read
But carry
For ever,

One blunt page, garlanded
By daughter
or lover.

You already know two-thirds by heart.
And I'm passing weighty for a work so short.

Riddles

Well: it's a riddle. It's also one of the better riddles in the language, so if you haven't figured out the answer yet, enjoy that delicious period of intrigued confusion for as long as you can. It's by no means very hard, though I confess it took me far longer than it should have; when I first read it, I was too beguiled by its music to worry much about the answer. However, I can think of no poem which better demonstrates the importance of the following advice: if you're stuck with a poem, *always* take the shortest route to literal sense. This is the reader's basic entitlement, but also generally the poet's intention, poets being far more literal-minded creatures than they are given credit for. If the poet asks you to *see* something – just try to visualize it, however crazy it sounds. Stop worrying about what it might stand for or symbolize. That will emerge – but from your intrigue, not your fretting about it.

So what have we here? In the tedious world of trope-analysis (it should bore everyone but poets, just as harmonic analysis should bore everyone but composers), symbols and riddles are structurally identical; however, unlike symbols, riddles often have concrete not abstract 'solutions'. In its presentation, a riddle is quite close to what we call 'a lie', and takes the form *X is Y*, where X is an unknown and Y a known. I love the perverse Western convention of using the first person in our riddles; this is partly because the declaration 'I am' is supposed to stand at the greatest distance from an untruth.

While you're thinking about it, a brief complaint. The problem with riddles is that unlike other kinds of poems they have 'correct' interpretations. When the answer is known, the poem is suddenly fixed – and no one wants to hear the same joke twice. This was the fatal flaw in the so-called 'Martian' School, which consisted of the literary critic Craig Raine plus 0.3 others. Their dubious creation was the 'single-use poem'. This was a matter of calling, say, a light bulb 'a pearl' (a bold similarity also arrived at independently by the light-bulb manufacturer, *Pearl*): dandy, as far as it goes. There's a little delay, the light goes on . . . and you go – 'Hey! It's not a pearl, it's a lightbulb. They *are* dashed similar, now that I think of it.' The next time you read it, alas, the light's already on and the fun is over. For this reason, the success of the riddle-poem depends on what *else* it's doing besides merely riddling us. Donaghy's riddle is not merely clever; it also has great wit, music and rhetorical power. Most poems are unstable signs in which we have the interpretative latitude to see ourselves; but riddles are different. You're not really 'allowed' to make of it what you will. Yet this poem seems to have both the broad resonance of a good poem, *and* a damn good solution.

Got it? It's *great* fun knowing the answer when someone else doesn't . . . Another fun thing is that when you *do* get the answer, you also get instant confirmation. The text replies *Yes! Yes!* However, if the riddle is more than a trivial visual pun, and the poet's hand has been concealed, the delay, the journey, the mini-pilgrimage you have to make *towards* the solution changes its nature; you'll never think of this thing in quite the same way again. It's a bit like taking a different route back to your own home address – not the usual way up the lane from the bus station, but through the woods, along the C-road, then cutting through the cemetery and your neighbours' back garden. This has the effect of letting us see the utterly familiar almost as if for the first time.

Any joy? OK: the trick with 'getting' riddles is firstly to forget about abstract solutions, because they're boring – and only a dull poet would have constructed one to which the answer was 'the mind', 'the soul', 'death' or 'the book of one's life'. So it's not that. The second thing is that *every* piece of evidence must fit perfectly, so you can't bleep over that *garland*, just because it doesn't fit 'birth certificate'. The third is that it won't be anything close to the bluff: here, the lie is that X is a 'book', so the answer will not be 'a diary'. (This is because riddles are forms of metaphors, and in a decent metaphor the comparison always has some element of surprise: so 'the can of Sprite looked just like a can of 7-Up' is not a great metaphor.) The fourth and most important bit of advice is to *paraphrase each line*, so that the clues are removed from the distracting context of the conceit itself. This not-book is just one page: one page of writing. A 'blunt page', too, which is an odd description, a page with its edges rounded. You won't or perhaps *can't* read it, but you will hold it above you for ever, which – as you won't live for ever – seems a bit odd. And flowers are laid upon this blunt-edged page by our nearest and dearest. There are three principal facts given on this page of writing, two of which are already in your possession: the last third is as yet unknown to you. And I'm exceedingly heavy (this use of 'passing' is archaic) for something so brief. I assume you've got it now – and lord knows you *will* get it, the poem reminds us, once you have just a little more information than your name and date of birth.

From the Safe House

I can just see Claire your good wife reading you this.
It has arrived this morning at your orchard in Vera Cruz
where your four brown daughters hector six chickens
and you lie beneath the dusty blue pickup
tying back the exhaust with a rusty hanger,
getting ready for the long haul north.

There are parts she skips, parts about her.
And parts I've yet to write or find a way to write.
The paper she reads from is yellowed, sharp-creased,
badly typed, postmarked Chicago, decades late,
from a Reagan winter, Pax Americana for Grenada,
the coldest winter of the life of the mind.

Soon I'll climb through snowdrifts to post it
from our clapboard student commune on the South Side
on a night six mummies dug from permafrost
huddle in coats breathing clouds in a room of books,
watching the last chair leg gutter on the grate
towards the heat death of its universe.

But for now it's still flickering, and Claire is beside me.
I'm too cold to talk, too cold to think, except of her.
I hear you hammer the ice from your boots on the porch
and the door slams back and you blow in from Urbana
from over the lake, from marching with steelworkers.
You look at the fire, the bookshelves, and make the first move.

Four highlighted copies of *One-Dimensional Man*,
old phone books, *Jaws*, *The Sensuous Woman* by J.
She's the first shovelled into the fire. You find it now,
hidden behind her, mimeographed, its staples gone to rust,
urgent and crumbly as this letter Claire's holding:
the *Manual of the Weather Underground*.

We'd been a safe house since '68 and never knew.
Did the Feds? Claire lets go my hand, takes it from you
and sniffs. Could it be any colder there?
Lit by flaring paperbacks and tequila she reads us,
like a bedtime story, the drill for evasion and escape.
I enclose it, with some photos of my son.

I have sent them you *then*, to the farm you planned,
to the heat haze in which you seem to waver,
where you lie beneath the same unsteerable wreck
your wife taught me to drive when you were drunk
and which I still own a seventh of, let's not forget,
(Tell him we never slept together, Claire)

instead of *now*, when I hear of your death,
after your stroke at my age give a month or two,
now, when you never made it to Mexico
and Claire remarried and never had children
and the clapboard safe house fell down at last
and the blue pickup went for scrap years back.

Dramatic monologue

In this short account of Donaghy's work I've no space to tackle 'Black Ice and Rain', an astonishing dramatic monologue in Donaghy's Wilbur-Browningesque mode. However, the shorter 'From The Safe House', the best poem in his posthumous collection *Safest*, is just as good. If on the basis of better-known poems like 'The Present' and 'Machines' you had gained the idea that Donaghy's stock-in-trade was the witty philosophical bagatelle, 'Black Ice and Rain' or this poem would dispel it. It's a narrative poem of great power and psychological insight, though one that sacrifices none of his Borgesian density. I find the best way to approach a fairly complex, longish poem like this is to first read it only for its shape and its flow, and just enjoy the story; then read it again, and focus on the detail.* By 'focussing on the detail' I mean 'as we do in a poem'. All we need to do is slow down our reading, and ask what every detail or image represents, either symbolically or metonymically (i.e. as evidence of a larger context). Poems like 'From The Safe House' achieve their density primarily by giving small pieces of information as evidence of larger events, emotions, ideas and domains. With a poet like Donaghy, one learns to trust that *any* detail, upon closer interrogation, will turn out

---

* Were I making a more technical analysis of this poem, I'd also look at the wide range of rhetorical devices Donaghy uses – but for most non-practising readers, such talk is not just unilluminating but counterproductive; the whole point about rhetorical effect is that it should do its work on the reader in an unseen, emotionally manipulative way. An effect swiftly identified is often one that isn't working.

to be the representative member of a much larger set, or stand for a broader context, or point to an unspoken cause; there are absolutely no lines of mere description or 'evocation'. In this way, a picture of novelistic depth can be built up in a tiny fraction of the space – but not without the reader's meticulous attention, on which its success depends.

To the poem. The principal difficulties of this poem relate to the (deictic) issues of chronological sequence and 'reality'. In a familiar self-descriptive, reflexive move, the poem doesn't describe the letter the speaker is sending, but *is* the letter itself. The author is a member of a commune of students or young adults in Chicago, in the winter of 1983. We can establish the year from the perfect 'relevant index' Donaghy provides, a political event that will have much detained them: the US invasion of Grenada, when Maurice Bishop's government fell to hardline pro-communists, and Ronald Reagan intervened; this event symbolizes the end, too, of their socialist idealism. The letter is addressed to a male member of the group to whom the speaker was close, though there's been a long rift in their relationship. (Though the speaker affects otherwise, it's also addressed to his friend's future wife, with whom he may have been in love.)

Although we don't discover this until the final stanza, the speaker is doing something magically impossible, and is speaking from two distinct times simultaneously (as in the poem 'Haunts', which follows): the present, and Chicago, 1983. The letter he is writing in 1983 will be sent that very night, in one of the most bitter winters in memory, to his friend in the future. (*On a night six mummies dug from permafrost* is not just a clever image of the freezing cold they endure, but a comment on how deep in time this memory has been dug out from.) Claire appears to be involved with both men, in that communal way; the speaker knows, however, that she will finally end up with his friend, whom he also seems to regard as the worthier party. This man walks the walk; while the rest of them were just trying to keep warm, he was out with striking steelworkers on a march in nearby Urbana.

The winter's so bad, the students are so broke and the house is so cold that they're burning the furniture. The speaker's unnamed friend returns, and seeing no alternative, begins to burn their library. Whatever the circumstances, this can't be a neutral gesture; here we might read it as 'burning the very ideals on which the community was founded'. The titles are all symbolically suggestive. Herbert Marcuse's *One-Dimensional Man* was something of an anti-capitalist bible, and addressed the decline of the revolutionary spirit in the West, which Marcuse claimed had been sapped by the Newspeak of mass media and advertising. (*Four copies* is a joke against itself, and suggests that the commune was rather sheep-like in its ideologies.) The classic sex manual, *The Sensuous Woman* by J. (the anonym of Joan Garrity), also goes in the flames. This might be construed as more of an aggressive act, and symbol of either misogyny or a barely disguised sexual jealousy.

Then behind *The Sensuous Woman* they make the key discovery. Looking like a letter from the long-ago past – hang on, just like this one – they find an ancient copy of *The Manual of the Weather Underground*. This was the handbook of the Weathermen, the group of left-wing insurgents who, inspired by Black Power and the anti-war campaigns of the 1960s, effectively declared war against the US government through a series of bombings of symbolic targets. And then it dawns on them: *We'd been a safe house since '68 and never knew.* The commune was a secret place of refuge for the Weathermen – not only a place where they cooked up their plots and bombs, but to which they could run for anonymous shelter when they were catching heat. *Did the Feds know?* The paranoia is typical of Donaghy. Perhaps they were being watched, still. Claire takes the manual and reads *the drill for evasion and escape*, and we sense that other exits are being planned too. It's as if *they* had rumbled their own safe house, whose refuge can no longer hold.

Maybe this was around the time Claire and his friend decided this youthful, utopian madness was unsustainable, and perhaps this night was the exact tipping point. Their own dream of their future together – and the poet's dream for them – is precisely the future reality into which this letter from the past arrives. Claire and the friend have a farm in Mexico; the communally owned, beloved old pickup truck is still being patched up, and they have four daughters, and six chickens. *Tell him we never slept together, Claire* addresses, it seems, the poisoning suspicion that had lingered and destroyed their friendship. (But why is he sending with this letter *the drill for evasion and escape* from the manual? The friend is already preparing the old truck for a journey back north over the border; has their dream been rumbled, and is the speaker trying to free them before their real fate catches up?)

But now the reason for the decades-late letter – its prompting, its urgency – becomes clear, with one of the most movingly bleak endings I have read since MacNeice's 'Soap Suds'. (That poem works, incidentally, through a similar syntactic effect.) The end of the poem is a bare, relentless list, an effect created by linking the phrases not through punctuation but conjunctions, and the hammered initial repetition of *and* (or what we could call a mixture of polysyndeton and anaphora). The future dream was just that and no more. The friend stroked out in his forties, never made it to Mexico, was divorced by Claire and died childless, and the blue pickup – the 'Rosebud' of this tale – *went for scrap years back*. Of course it did. *The Safe House* did not keep them safe, yet the letter is an act of wish-fulfilment (as well as confession and restitution) from a 'safe' place in the past into a future which might yet be protected by it. Perhaps if this letter could only reach its destination, it might still be met with that better reality?

The poem is eight stanzas of six lines, making forty-eight; this was Donaghy's age at the time of the poem's composition, and, we can assume, that of his former brother-in-arms. If he was real. Donaghy conspicuously did not offer the usual strenuous denials when I asked him about the autobiographical origins of this poem (the line *I enclose it, with some photos of my son* seems to break the fourth wall); it's fair to surmise that some, at least, of this riveting, tragic middle-aged novella of a poem may have been drawn from life.*

---

* Maddy Paxman assures me that this was indeed the case, and that many of the details are genuine; the poem was written on hearing of his friend's death. The house on South Kenwood Avenue is still standing. However, 1983 was one of the mildest Chicago winters on record. Facts are useful in poems right up to the point that they start interfering with the truth.

Haunts

Don't be afraid, old son, it's only me,
though not as I've appeared before,
on the battlements of your signature,
or margin of a book you can't throw out,
or darkened shop front where your face
first shocks itself into a mask of mine,
but here, alive, one Christmas long ago
when you were three, upstairs, asleep,
and haunting *me* because I conjured you
the way that child you were would cry out
waking in the dark, and when you spoke
in no child's voice but out of radio silence,
the hall clock ticking like a radar blip,
a bottle breaking faintly streets away,
you said, as I say now, *Don't be afraid*.

December 27 1999

Time and tense

This is an involute and haunted 4-D Chinese box of a poem, written in a single sentence. The last poem in *Conjure*, the last collection to be published in the poet's lifetime, it reads exactly like his last word. Typically, it tries to offer the listener some sense of safety and comfort; from a man so perennially unsafe and uncomforted, this strikes me as especially heartbreaking. Its syntax is meticulous, and meticulously complex. If you miss one cue regarding point-of-view or tense, or misread a single function word – confusion will ensue. But it's all laid out for us, and it's important that it *does* read as though several dimensions have been balled up into a very small space, since that's exactly what the poem seeks to prove: that linear time, which appears to do little but separate us from each other, is just an illusion.

We might first assume that the poem is written in the voice of the poet's own father speaking from beyond the grave, but only because this is a less radical interpretation than the one the poem actually demands: it soon becomes clear that we're listening to the voice of the poet himself – only he's dead, and speaking from the future. This information is given most clearly by the distance between the tense in which the poem is written, and the date of its composition. This 'final poem' is the *only* one Donaghy ever dated, making this fact crucially significant: two days after Christmas 1999. This serves three functions, all of which constrain and direct the sense. The first is to make sure we identify this date with the Christmas mentioned in the poem. The second is to name the year that would also, were we to research the matter, prove the autobiographical authenticity of this poem: we could confirm that Ruairí Tomás was three years old in 1999. The third is to introduce the vertiginous idea that the 'present' might not be constituted as we think it is. This poem seeks to dismantle it as a consistent concept.

The key to understanding the poem is to bear in mind that the title is plural, and read it as belonging to two different times at once, connected by a kind of temporal wormhole. It's written and dated by the poet in the here-and-now – but it is also spoken by the poet's own ghost to the older son he will not live to see become a man. (Donaghy's awareness of his own impending demise seemed to quicken by the year; it was literally ticking away in the back of his head, a congenital flaw which seems to have taken his mother at almost exactly the same age.) The poem also reflects and inverts the first poem in *Conjure*, 'The Excuse', where the living son and the dead father also haunt each other; a haunting is an interfusion of souls. 'My people were magicians . . .' This, too, is a conjuring. The poet is summoning both his own voice from the future – and from that *same* future, that of his own grown son.

. . . *old son, it's only me* picks up on the epigraph to *Conjure*, the moment in *Hamlet* when his father's ghost first appears:

> Horatio: *It beckons you to go away with it*
> *As if it some impartment did desire*
> *To you alone*
>
> *Only me, old son.*

The ghost-father's colloquial, carefully non-scary greeting is of course Donaghy's addition, and has the sweet tone of an old Ealing comedy, until you notice the odd, near-oxymoron of 'old son'. The poem makes great play with this phrase. *It's only me*, a friendly presence; I'm *present*. The voice of the dead poet now addresses the grown son, in a time far in the future. He says, 'I'm not the kind of ghost you think I am, son – the one you know from the mirror of the darkened shop front, the annotations in my old books, in the shape of your own handwriting. I'm the sort that speaks directly, and audibly, exactly as when I was alive.'

The battlements of your signature is a breathtaking metaphor. It's visually clever, certainly; signatures can look like crenellations on a castle, and also it sends us back to the place Hamlet meets his dead father. It's also a symbol of the heritable. Despite the signature being the classic mark of our individuation, our handwriting styles are often influenced by our parents. It's also making a quieter comment on the often defensive nature of selfhood.

The next few clauses form a complex proposition –

> but here, alive, one Christmas long ago
> when you were three, upstairs, asleep,
> and haunting *me* because I conjured you
> the way that child you were would cry out
> waking in the dark,

– *but here, alive, one Christmas long ago* refers to the time and place this poem is being composed – December 1999, when the father was alive, yet the ghost is also speaking in the far future. (This is a similar 'wormhole' technique to that employed by the speaker in 'From The Safe House'.) Then the explanation is given. In Christmas 1999, the child is haunting the *father*. The infant son is upstairs asleep, at some small distance from where the father is sitting. Yet the living father has conjured up the child as though summoning a friendly ghost – and he does so out of immense fear, just the way that his own child sometimes wakes terrified in the dark, calling out for his parents.

But when the child answers . . . it's in *no child's voice*. His conjured speech also comes from the future: the voice is disembodied, and arrives through the eerie, empty wavebands, the white noise of radio silence, of the broadcast of nothing alive, with no sound but the end of a party streets away. (There's also one of Donaghy's marvellous composite machines, the hall clock that is also radar scanning for alien or ghostly presences. Remember, too, Donaghy's favourite symbol: white noise as a signifier of the beyond.) He hears the voice of the *old son* his son will be when the poet himself is a ghost. And that voice from the future now comforts the living father, here, in 1999 – a man living in terror of the death he knows is coming for him soon enough. But not only can the *old son* tell him *don't be afraid*; proof is given that time is illusory, and cannot kill love. And now the living father is in possession of that evidence, he can pass those words on to the son in the future, when he is old enough to hear them, and perhaps need them.

Don't be afraid. The *old son*'s words of comfort for his father are simultaneously spoken, quoted and also borrowed by the ghost. The poem has one of the most complex and sophisticated relationships to the concepts of time and tense of any I know, but its apparent illogic is really a proof. In 'Burnt Norton' from *Four Quartets*, Eliot writes: *Time present and time past / Are both perhaps present in time future / And time future contained in time past. / If all time is eternally present / All time is unredeemable.* To which this poem adds: 'Yes – but *we* are redeemed by this circumstance.'

Donaghy seems to have been vouchsafed the information *there is no death*, and is keen to let us know. His fears were about living, and for the living. Death, by contrast, is where we are safest. *Don't be afraid.* These are the words uttered by better souls on their deathbeds, concerned not for themselves but for the comfort of the living: the dead don't require quite the same reassurances. (*Noli timere* was what Seamus Heaney texted his wife shortly before his own death.) As is so often the case with Donaghy, there is also poetry in the form itself. It's a sonnet – but a *fifteen*-line sonnet (iambic, switching lightly between a four-strong line and i.p.), where the last line doubles and alters the first.

In the warmest and most human way imaginable, this offers a little 'closure', both for readers of this poem and for those who still grieve for the man himself. The poem 'closes its own circle' – but does so like a Mobius strip. We are never really alone; we haunt one another too well.

Disquietude

Would you know it if our phone was tapped?
Would you hear a series of clicks, for example?
Or the sound of breathing? Or policemen typing?
After the next caller hangs up stay on the line.
Stay on until you're sure.

One day when we were younger and hornier
I stashed a tape recorder underneath our bed. Please don't be angry.
I wanted to keep the noises we made when we weren't ourselves,
but all the mic picked up was wheezing springs. Just as well.
It would be like listening to strangers now.

Our names have sounds besides the ones we hear.
Sometimes, when I wake beside you in the night
and the door of sleep slams shut and locks behind me,
I hear it creep up out of silence, a brash hush,
a crowded emptiness, the static of the spheres.

It's like a tap left on. But it's my own warm blood,
the flood that's washing all the names away,
of schoolmates, kings, the principal export of somewhere,
and all the sounds as well – a lullaby, a child's voice –
my own warm blood that must be blessed.

No recording devices are allowed in this hall.
The lights dim, and onstage they're coughing,
turning pages, giving the score their indivisible attentions,
getting settled for the next movement
which features no one and is silent.

Voice

No one except Donaghy could have written this poem, and while I am moved and disturbed by it, I intend that first statement neutrally. This is a poem which suffers a little from self-impersonation, a hazard every poet with a strong style will encounter later in their career. A number of Donaghy's last poems are too much like this: half-mad with fear and paranoia, riddled with foreboding and danger. This one contains almost all of his signature obsessions: surveillance, music, audio capture technology, error, sleep, dreams, white noise, hypochondria, corporeality, and a Shakespearian awareness of the obliterating power of time. And, of course, death. Hardly worth mentioning, since, as Billy Collins has observed, death is what gets poets out of bed in the morning; Donaghy had been writing about it for ever. As is often the case with a great writer, signature themes gain in symbolic force when read in the context of their work as a whole. (By contrast, I'll also look at a poem which I think is diminished by this context.) This poem tap-dances on the abyss of self-impersonation, but just gets away with it. However, almost every line has already appeared in some other Donaghy poem in a different form.

The first stanza establishes some necessary deictic information very economically. It's the present; we're at home; it's addressed to his partner. It expresses the author's considerable worries over his own surveillance. (What exactly does he have to worry about?) The second stanza sees him make a confession: not only did he tape them making love, but the noises they made *when we weren't ourselves* were silent – at least as far the tape recorder was concerned; they couldn't be captured in this way. (As he later makes clear, we are to consider those sounds 'beyond ourselves' about as easy to record as the dead.) Who they *were* when they made love were people so distant in time as to be strangers; a terribly sad thought that most people in long-term relationships are likely to have shared at some point.

Then it gets weird. Sometimes, when he is alone beside his sleeping partner, locked out of the possibility of sleep, he hears white noise. This is such a well-established Donaghy symbol, it becomes a 'symbol' more in the Peircean than the literary sense. Donaghy-world reinforces a semi-arbitrary association between the appearance of white noise and the presence of the beyond, just as, say, we come to associate 'yew tree' with 'death' in Sylvia Plath. We hear it in 'Exile's End' and in 'Haunts', for example; I suspect it is *the voice of many waters* in 'The Tuning'; elsewhere it is present as strong sibilance – *while amethyst uraeuses of flame / Hissed above us* in 'Pentecost'. (I have a hunch it may originate with the untuned television in Spielberg's *Poltergeist*.) This is the sound that lies behind the limits of our known being: not the *music* of the spheres, but the loud *shhhh* of them. The sound is also like running water; but a tap left running is an error, and can lead to flooding, very much of the sort we see in 'The River in Spate', where the mistake is falling asleep. But it's the sound (as John Cage observes in 'Cage') of his own nervous system, his own being. And as our hearts beat blood round our bodies, they also beat time away, and with it everything that we learn as a secure fact, everything we memorize. *My own warm blood that must be blessed* is a strange line that partly defeats me, but it probably refers to the kind of auto-communion we encounter in 'The Brother'.

At the end of many poems, we often make a simultaneous deictic shift to an elsewhere and an 'elsewhen';* but as I've discussed, there's an extra aspect to poetic deixis. Not just *who? when? where?* But *is it real?* No, we've made a shift, and *this hall* is a metaphor. It represents the hushed hall of death, of unrecordable, beyond-self no-sound, of static and silence that forms our most intimate small-hours encounter with the beyond, the eternal. There's a great performance about to begin, and as in 'Exile's End' the orchestra are 'doing the very last thing', preparing, clearing their throats, and finding their place in the score. *Indivisible attentions* is, I believe, a crucial pun: *indivisible* because they are concentrated solely on the music, yes – but *indivisible* because they are one, again, like the voice of 'Exile's End': a coral-like non-human consciousness, an indivisible *we* beyond the world dominated by the misery of the single-organism, individuated, ego-bound human.

But what comes is a *tutti tacit*, essentially Cage's 4′33″ arranged for full orchestra. (This exists, incidentally; in its way, it's rather wonderful, and somehow much louder than the original.) Only *this* movement is literally endless, and the only way you will ever experience it is played live. Ironic, given your circumstances.

---

* Or an 'elsewho', or a metapoetic shift – or some combination of all or any of them. This is a feature so common and fundamental to poetic closure, I have a PhD student writing an entire thesis on what she calls 'closural shift theory'.

Local 32B

(US National Union of Building Service Workers)

The rich are different. Where we have doorknobs,
they have doormen – like me, a cigar store Indian
on the Upper East Side, in polyester, in August.
As the tenants tanned in Tenerife and Monaco
I stood guard beneath Manhattan's leaden light
watching poodle turds bake grey in half an hour.
Another hot one, Mr Rockefeller!
An Irish doorman foresees his death,
waves, and runs to help it with its packages.
Once I got a cab for Pavarotti. No kidding.
No tip either. I stared after him down Fifth
and caught him looking after me, then through me,
like Samson, eyeless, at the Philistine chorus –
Yessir, I put the tenor in the vehicle.
And a mighty tight squeeze it was.

The personal perspective

Donaghy is dead, which is mostly a downer, but at least I don't have to listen to him telling me I stole his jokes any more. *Au contraire*, Mikey: I gave you the frankly brilliant *An Irish doorman foresees his death** line in a Turkish restaurant in London – I recall it vividly because I was so pleased with myself at the time. Although I accept that the addition of . . . *waves, and runs to help it with its packages* improves it immensely. Despite his hysterical claims to the contrary, my even more hilarious line on Rilke's 'Archaic Torso of Apollo' ('You must lose some weight') was not his either. I think. False accusations of theft may not be the sincerest form of flattery, but I'll still take them. That's not to say I wasn't averse to stealing from *his* conversation mercilessly, but the dead can't sue, and besides, we all did it.

This is a piece of light verse, and a poem drawn from the poet's own experience. It's unrhymed, and in a free-ish, medium-length line that makes the odd playful nod to i.p. Donaghy worked as a doorman on Park Avenue as a young man. Michael was a very handsome guy, but also a very sweaty one. He was once banned from the posh gym in one of the buildings he concierged for dripping all over the equipment. I own a coat of his he wore for years; its sweat-stink, now a full ten years old, will outlive us all and survive the heat death of the cosmos. What polyester in a New York August would have

---

* . . . adapting Yeats, but you knew that. As part of his reading shtick, Donaghy would sometimes unsmilingly gloss everything, until the audience got the joke. 'Dante, the noted Italian poet . . .'

done to him, I shudder to think. While he was on duty, he used to keep a slim volume hidden in his cap; when no one was around, he'd take off his hat and read a couple of poems on the sly. This was not without risk. New York doormen are proud professionals with a union many would kill to join, and go about their responsibilities with deadly earnestness – as anyone will testify who has ever tried to stroll into an Upper West Side elevator before being buzzed up. One day he was caught reading by a wealthy resident, and was worried she'd report him to the union for his crime. He needn't have; they immediately struck up a conversation about the Hopkins he was reading, and she turned out to be the treasurer of the famous reading series at the 92nd Street Y. We can assume that Michael charmed the pants off her. She ended the conversation by giving him a subscription to the Poetry Center as a gift. Donaghy had never been to a poetry reading before, but within a month, he'd seen Borges and Basil Bunting, and everything changed for him.

This is a just a joke-poem, really, and we shouldn't interrogate it for any deeper meaning. Michael loved jokes – or at least the same fifteen jokes which he would tell over and over again, faster at every repetition. Those who were lucky or unfortunate enough to have heard his infamous performance of 'The Pope and the Rabbi' (punchline: 'and then we had lunch') will know what I mean. He would often arrive late – actually he would *always* arrive late – to a social gathering with what appeared to be a great excuse. Once he showed up all shirt-tailed, unshowered and panic-stricken, and told us that he'd been with the police all afternoon. After a week abroad, he'd returned to his flat to find it had been broken into, and that they'd taken everything. We all expressed our dismay and great concern. 'But the really weird thing was they'd replaced it with *completely identical stuff* – only slightly dustier.'

The last two lines of this poem are a cheap-but-great in-house gag, punning on I. A. Richards's now-standard terms 'tenor' and 'vehicle' for the two parts of a metaphor (the subject, and the thing to which the subject is compared). One cannot logically put the tenor in the vehicle, and cramming a very fat singer into a yellow cab is just as tricky. You can sense the gleeful violence with which the author did so, however, after Pavarotti has stared through him like the *Philistine*, uncultured oaf he no doubt assumed his doorman to be. There's a little metapoetic joke here: this poem *would* have been a sonnet but for Pavarotti's bulk, and an extra line is required to fit the big guy in.

I know some reading this little commentary might find my tone a bit too chatty, personal and subjective for 'proper literary criticism', but it's important to remind ourselves that *no one* gets to say what literary criticism is. It's for no one else to tell us what we can or cannot adduce to shed light on what we read. There are many lights, and they all reveal something different. Some are colder and academic, some are warmer and more personal. Some are overhead, some sidelong, some are diffuse, and some are laser-sharp; some are like the white blast of a Xerox and some like the thin greenish glow cast by Venus on a new moon. But if you shine just *one* light on a poem, there's one thing guaranteed: you will find more or less exactly what you set out to discover.

So if you're reading a poem, and happen to know anything about the author – me, I'd just use it. Not exclusively, not disproportionately, not injudiciously – and not as if it holds any secret key to the true meaning of the poem, or trumps a sensible close reading: it most assuredly doesn't. But use it. A poem is many things, but at heart it's just a conversation between two monkeys. The critical practice of insisting that the biographical or personal perspective must *always* be suppressed is essentially pretending that the author was not human, and that you aren't either.

Hazards

1

Once upon a time there was a dark blue suit.
And one fine morning the chamberlain laid it out upon a bed
and the ministers of state assembled round it singing
God preserve and protect the emperor!

2

Don't worry. I gave the dancing monkey your suicide note.
Was it something important? How was I to know?
He's probably torn it to pieces by now or eaten it
or substituted every word for one adjacent in the dictionary.

3

And suddenly there came a sound from heaven as of a
    rushing mighty wind,
and cloven tongues like as of fire sat upon the heads of the
    disciples
and they began to speak with other tongues
in order to confound the multitude.

4

Was it the white pine face like a new moon?
The wet splutter and moan of the shakuhachi?
Was it the actor's dispersal in gesture and smoke?
What part of Noh did you not understand?

The avant-garde

Michael did not much like the avant-garde. This is Donaghy's lightly encoded rant against those he saw as art's obscurantists – 'the ampersands', as he called them* – and very funny it is too. Like most of us, Michael was something of a coward, in that the distance between his privately and publicly expressed opinions was often considerable. I doubt he needs our protection now, and this little poem seems explicitly vicious enough anyway. In a sort of poetry version of the Sokal hoax, he would occasionally submit and publish poems in avant-garde journals, all composed with an egg-timer. They were usually acrostic sonnets that read ARRANT NONSENSE or UTTER BULLSHIT. (A few others were signed by his French alter ego, the *ampersandeuse* Hélène-Marie Journod, though some of those were actually pretty good.) He swore he once had found that the homepage for an online *avant* site had been taken down, and replaced by the highly poetic holding notice: 'this website is temporarily closed due to a hoax poem'. Which is one of the funniest things I've ever heard, and if that isn't Russell's Paradox I don't know what is, or possibly isn't. He had an imaginary journal of experimental poetry called

---

* . . . from the fondness certain poets have for using '&' instead of 'and'. The usual defence is that since 'and' is just a functional marker, it's barely spoken, and so might as well be represented by a shorthand. The usual objection is: a) that's true of almost every other function word; b) it has the opposite effect to the one intended, i.e. it does nothing but draw attention to itself – and that this is precisely the idea, since it's more a sign of ideological allegiance than a typographical convenience.

The Hierophant: a Journal of Post-Vorticist Verse. Hierophant posters would occasionally appear. These might advertise anything from a seminar on Amy Lowell and Deleuzian assemblage to pleas for the return of a lost poodle.

Hazards? Obstacles, risks . . . though the title refers primarily to the game of dice, or chance (the word is probably from the Arabic *al zar*, a die). He was perplexed by the kind of randomizing procedures employed by some poets of the L=A=N=G=U=A=G=E school, and how those rules could possibly produce poetry of any kind. The poem itself takes four cultural clichés, shakes them up and rolls them out again.

With its *once upon a time* and *one fine morning*, the first stanza inverts the Hans Christian Andersen fairy-tale of the two naughty tailors who fashion a suit for the Emperor, which they claim will be invisible to the stupid and the incompetent. No one, of course, will admit that they can't see it – until a kid cries out that the king is naked. The 'emperor's new clothes' is an accusation hurled at anything perceived to be all hype, whose alleged novel brilliance is nothing but delusion and wishful thinking. All too often it's hurled by someone who hasn't quite understood that they've put themselves in an equally presumptuous position – that of the clear-eyed child in the story, the noble truth-teller standing up against the cowardly or self-deluded herd who have overpraised a mediocrity, or found the new in the same old, same old. Donaghy will have heard this insult thrown at 'the mainstream' any time a new talent was claimed or celebrated. (In the ten years since his death, things have become considerably less tribal, mainly owing to the wiser influence of a younger generation who just can't see or care what we were all fighting about.)

The mainstream tend to regard the avants as similarly

stuck: stuck to an ideal of innovation for its own sake, of meretricious novelty, endlessly repeated. (In Auden's or Valéry's or someone's timeless remark: 'everything changes but the avant-garde'.) In this inverted parable, the empty jacket and pants are praised as if the emperor were still inside them. There's a fine new suit there all right – but there's no one inside it; it's all style and no substance. A flash new suit of novel strategies, maybe, but with no *poem* inside; lots of intertextuality, but – Darn! I knew we'd forgotten something – no text.

In the second stanza we're asked to think of Aesop's fable of the dancing monkeys. A prince trains chimps to mimic dancers, and dresses them up as courtiers. All goes well until someone throws them a handful of nuts – and they revert to monkeys again, tearing off their fancy clothes and scrapping on the floor. In the end, monkeys will be monkeys. But who is *this* monkey? Well, one who substitutes every word with one adjacent in the dictionary – which turns out to be a metonym for 'the avant-garde' again. This is a well-known aleatoric device: you take a poem, or you write a poem, and then you substitute every content word for the next one in the OED. Or shall we say . . . you takhi a po-faced, or wrizled a po-faced, and then you subtract every conterminal wore for the next unrelaxed one in the dictum. (Much 'linguistically innovative' verse comes out like a sketch from *The Two Ronnies*.) Along with homophonic translation, collages and hyper-intertextuality, these parlour games can offer the poet hours and hours of harmless fun. But for the *reader*, Donaghy suggests, it's funless harm: that suicide note, that precious scrap of tormented human emotion that the monkey had somehow been vouchsafed? Yes, it probably *was* something important. But it's too late, now the monkey has it. Monkeys do what monkeys do.

Pervert, cut up, destabilize, decentre, fracture, fragment and problematize. Gah! Sorry about that. (I'm confused by the speaker here – who *is* this irresponsible go-between? The critic?)

The third stanza takes as its subject a Donaghy favourite – the miracle at Pentecost, described in Acts 2. This makes minimal changes to the King James Version, but if you read it in the context of its emerging 'thematic domain' (otherwise known as 'what you now suspect the poem is about') – the whole sense has been hideously inverted. Yes, the gathered multitude are confounded all right – but not as in 'stunned', and not because 'every man heard them speak in his own language'. We are now directed to read *other tongues* as 'tongues not their own', i.e. tongues that made no damn sense at all. This is the anti-apostles' purpose – to *confuse* the multitude. There was no doubt in Donaghy's mind that avant-garde practice had done precisely that: claimed a poetic inspiration, but delivered a poetry wholly inaccessible to the vast majority of intelligent readers.

The final stanza is an exquisite bad joke. 'What part of "no" don't you understand?' is a standard, angry rhetorical question made in response to a stupid repeated request. Here, it's recast as a patronizing, faux-concerned query posed to a bewildered non-initiate – one wholly unversed in the locked, weird rules and tropes of Japanese Noh theatre. 'Ah yes: you cannot understand the deep truth of this art unless you are as fluent in its complex traditions and symbols as I am.' But what the speaker is really delivering is a refusal, a no-entry sign. *This isn't for you.* The message of the whole poem, however, is a defiant 'You can keep it.'

Irena of Alexandria

Creator, thank You for humbling me.
Creator, who twice empowered me to change
a jackal to a saucer of milk,
a cloud of gnats into a chandelier,
and once, before the emperor's astrologers,
a nice distinction into an accordion,
and back again, thank You
for choosing Irena to eclipse me.

She changed a loaf of bread into a loaf of bread,
caused a river to flow downstream,
left the leper to limp home grinning and leprous,
because, the bishops say, Your will burns
bright about her as a flame about a wick.

Thank You, Creator, for taking the crowds away.
Not even the blind come here now.
I have one bowl, a stream too cold to squat in,
and the patience of a saint. Peace be,
in the meantime, upon her. And youth.
May sparrows continue to litter her shoulders,
children carpet her footsteps in lavender,
and may her martyrdom be beautiful and slow.

Jealousies

This is a dramatic monologue set, I assume, round the time of the Church Fathers. The speaker is a miracle-working anchorite who, prior to the arrival of the competition, thought he was nicely on the road to beatitude. The trouble with the saintly path is that you have to maintain the pose, even when it's going very badly. As a supplicant to God's will, he must thank his Creator for both his fortune and his misfortune, since it's all part of His plan; but his teeth are so tightly clenched they're about to splinter. The result is a very funny speech on the subject of professional jealousy, and a revealing insight into the shop-floor politics of the career mystic. (I think it's significant that most men hear this poem as spoken by a man, and most women by a woman. It seems to touch the kind of chord that has us make our interpretations as close to home as possible.)

His frustration seems justified: he's performed some fine miracles, albeit rather useless and random ones. The *nice distinction* is used in the rather archaic sense of a subtle, precise, and therefore small difference.

So what did Irena (whose name means, irritatingly, 'peace') do to provoke all this jealousy? Literally nothing at all: she really *is* the emperor's new clothes, loud and proud. She did God's will, and performed the super-humble miracle of leaving things exactly as they are, which is presumably the way that God prefers them. The only surprise is that everyone is so grateful for the experience: even the leper is suddenly, joyously resigned to his condition. And how can she possess such grace? *Because, the bishops say, Your will burns / bright about her as a flame about a wick*. Our man doesn't say it, however. (I hear those lines as being thrown away with stock-phrase contempt. If one were to try and seek out a more serious agenda here, we might think of Irena as the perfect poet, in the context of Viktor Shklovsky's statement that 'art exists that one may recover the sensation of life; it exists to make one feel things, to make the stone stony', and his famous idea of *ostranenie* or defamiliarization. I'm not sure this poem is 'really about poetry', though, for all it may well be about poets. Mainly it's just a gas.)

And for Irena's reliable gift of revealing the world as the world, the crowds have flocked to her. The speaker should be happy, though: through God's will, he's been returned to a state of ascetic perfection – of immaculate privation and solitude, and all the time in the world to meditate. *The patience of a saint* is, of course, delivered with withering sarcasm, as he's watching his sainthood slip away from him, but he's praying God is deaf to tone. Then he rises above himself to wish Irena all the best, especially in the matter of her martyrdom, which we can be certain he keenly awaits. Professional jealousy is endemic to all walks of life, but maybe it needs a bitch-off between two early Christian mystics to really hammer home how ridiculous it is.

This is another of Donaghy's Fibonacci poems. Stanzas of eight, five, and eight lines make a twenty-one-line form, breaking down into something like a thirteen-line sonnet and an octave.

Meridian

There are two kinds of people in the world.
Roughly. First there are the kind who say
'There are two kinds of people in the world'
And then there's those who don't.

Me, I live smack on the borderline,
Where the road ends with towers and searchlights,
And we're kept awake all night by the creak of the barrier
Rising and falling like Occam's razor.

Paradox

The poet did his best to make this poem look like a squib. However, not only is it a profound logical conundrum right up there with Gödel – Donaghy's Paradox is also a moral one, and asks us to examine the nature of judgement itself. Everything in this poem is deliberately twin-sensed and two-faced. The meridian is an imaginary line that runs through the poles and divides the earth, and where we divide the day at noon. The poem is about division, dividers, and the divided mind, and is divided into two equal parts.

The poem starts with an old joke, along the lines of 'there are 10 kinds of people in the world: those who understand binary, and those who don't'. But the poet subverts the joke from the start, and has it nest its own paradox within itself. There *can't* be *two kinds of people in the world.* / *Roughly.* Either there are or there aren't. But between the two opening lines, the speaker has switched between the tongues in which a border-dweller must be fluent. The first is the voice of certainty, the kind that can make clean distinctions, and say bold things like 'there are two kinds of people in the world'. 'Roughly' is the second kind, the far less sure. To live *on the borderline* means to live, as we all do, between certainty and equivocation, between the delivered verdict and the withheld judgement. So what if you're both kinds of people? We all are. We judge and we refuse to; we equivocate between certainty and equivocation itself. This dithering about whether to dither, Donaghy points out, is an infinite regress.

The rule of Occam's razor states that the most economical solution, the one which makes fewest assumptions, is the one most likely to be true. The barrier of Occam's razor is rigorously, relentlessly trying to minimize the propositions – which keep multiplying because the border is the land of uncertain possibility: so Occam's barrier is never done with its rising and falling, rising and falling, as it tries to simplify the swithering migrants from the dark land beyond. But who passes through this barrier? The equivocators and the certain, wandering back and forth? And might they be caught under the barrier's constant attempts to make its clean distinctions, falling like a giant guillotine? Whatever this difference is, it's important enough – enough of an 'intellectual nationality' – to have some intimidating border patrols.

The trouble with Occam's razor is that it doesn't always work. It's more a rule of style than logic: the simplest solutions aren't always the truest. As Einstein instructed us, you should make it as simple as you can, *but no simpler*. Simplifications sooner or later become lies and misrepresentations. Those who take the simplistic position that there are two kinds of people in the world consider themselves one or the other, and the other soon becomes the alien, the not-like-us. And there are no others, in the eyes of absolutists, quite like those relativists who will not make up their minds. Some rail against the Scottish justice system for this reason – and from their judgemental perspective, the third verdict of *not proven* will never make any sense: you're either guilty or you aren't. But knowledge isn't perfect. We aren't actually *compelled* to make our decisions based on our nice, clean binary distinctions; we're either inclined to or we aren't. Maybe.

A Messenger

With no less purpose than the swifts
that scrawl my name across the sky,
the hand of an obsessed pianist
quivers inches from my face.

She's anchored so she hangs mid-air
like an angel in a Christmas play.
As fidgety, but tinier, and she's forgot
her only line, *Fear not*.

With no less purpose
than her prey, the fritillary,
flicks a wing and swells the Yangtze,
she's spun a filament across my path.

I could no more cross this line
and wreck her morning's work
than graph the plot that brought me
eye to compound eye with her.

I'd worry for her, out so far
on such tenuous connections,
but the crosshairs of the gunsight
are implied in her precision.

Fate

Always read the poet's opening proposition carefully; it often contains the whole poem in microcosm. One might not think of swifts as having much *purpose*, but the kind that write your name in the air . . . Those are different. The more crucial point, of course, is what it tells us about the speaker, who is less an unreliable witness as one who may be losing his mind – but perhaps no more than any of us will when we're at our morbidly solipsistic worst. The swifts, of course, have no such intent. The purposeful spider is brilliantly described as a disembodied hand of a pianist, practising 'air arpeggios'. (*Obsessed* is an epithet transferred from the speaker's own state of mind.) Then the little spider-messenger takes a different form: she's like a fidgety angel in a school nativity play, suspended from the ceiling, and the *message* is the annunciation: alas, our little Gabriel forgets his only line, *Fear not*. The spider-Gabriel not only fails to comfort – the message is presumably *be very afraid*, by omission. The spider's prey, either present or intended, is a fritillary butterfly. The cliché of chaos theory is that a tiny, chance event like a butterfly flapping its wings can trigger a chain reaction that results in catastrophic, massive atmospheric changes. Donaghy knows fine well that 'fritillary' is derived from the Latin *fritillus*, a dice-box. However, the speaker claims that the dice are loaded, and that the swollen Yangtze river is part of the butterfly's own deliberate design; a butterfly with this kind of *purpose* would reveal not just a wholly deterministic universe, but one populated by an infinite number of agents; this reveals the speaker as a kind of paranoid fatalist. The web of fate has its weavers, and like the butterfly's wing, *this* web will have its remote and terrible consequences too.

The poet now declares that he could no more destroy the spider's web than outline the fatal net of forces that brought them eye to eye in the first place. He is helpless against the machinations of fate – even tenderly protective of them. As Borges said, in many different ways – there *is* such a thing as fate; its machinery is just far too complex for us to apprehend. Just so, the spider is far from the killing centre of her web – but even out here on the edge, in her minuscule adjustments to local tensions, the whole is still implied. Donaghy uses the visual metaphor of the gunsight, often represented as a cross through concentric circles. In comparing it to the web, he also suggests that our precise fixing of the enemy is a natural motif. ('Range-Finding' by Frost works through a similarly chilling visual pun on webs and target-practice.) *Messenger*: one who carries a message, a thing sent. If he was merely a paranoiac, the message our little spider would have for this guy is 'they're out to get you'. Alas, this guy is mad, and has added fatalism to the mix; this upgrades the warning to 'they're *going* to get you'.

Not Knowing the Words

Before he wearied of the task, he sang a nightly Mass
for the repose of the souls of the faithful departed
and magicked his blood to bourbon and tears
over the ring, the lock of hair, the dry pink dentures.
Was he talking to her? I never learned.
Walk in, he'd pretend to be humming softly,
like wind through a window frame.

The last I saw of him alive, he pressed me to his coat.
It stinks in a sack in my attic like a drowned Alsatian.
It's his silence. Am I talking to him now, as I get it out
and pull its damp night down about my shoulders?
Shall I take up the task, and fill its tweedy skin?
Do I stand here not knowing the words
when someone walks in?

Seances

This elegy for the poet's father is another evenly divided sonnet. The convention of breaking between the eighth and ninth line is so strong that most poets regard splitting it into two seven-line stanzas as daringly *asymmetrical*; it's almost a sin against the holy ghost. In this poem, the father performs a familiar Donaghy transubstantiation, turning his blood to wine (or whiskey, here) as he tries to commune with his dead wife. He has pride, and he's careful that he is never overheard. Talking to the recently dead is what we do, out of habit or desperation, until we get tired of them not talking back. Such is the poet's own confusion and ambivalence towards this exercise, he can't decide if this is the correct or perhaps even necessary procedure, and barely knows if he's already doing it.

I've always felt that the acquisition of 'object permanence' – the child's realization that things persist in their being, even when they disappear from sight – is a mixed blessing. When you understand that your mum hasn't died or disappeared every time she goes to the bathroom, you don't feel orphaned next time it happens. But when they *do* leave the room for ever, our minds suddenly have to process something they've learned to regard as a logical impossibility. Things *don't* just disappear. Alas, what we fail to learn is that we're not really 'things'; the table, that painting, that vase, this big coat – are all far more permanent than the soft machine that briefly houses our own ghost. Unable to accept the fact, we go on talking to no one, for a while at least. Maybe it's a service we perform for the dead; perhaps it really *is* the task of conducting their still-earthbound souls to the other side, and far more important than we know. If we are loved, our own bereaved will do this for us too; they will sit in rooms alone, quietly talking to us like lunatics. But the paradox for the living, for the left, is that all we have to invoke the dead are silent relics, tokens which often do little but *reinforce* their absence. Teeth, hair, rings, photos; a pair of broken spectacles; the old black gilet I'm wearing as I type this. What else are we meant to do? Let's face it, this situation is an embarrassment.

Our Life Stories

What did they call that ball in *Citizen Kane*?
That crystal blizzardball forecasting his past?
Surely I know the name. Your mum's souvenir
of Blackpool, underwater, in winter –
say we dropped it. What would we say we broke?
And see what it says when you turn it over . . .

I dreamt the little Christmas dome I owned
slipped my soapy fingers and exploded.
Baby Jesus and the Virgin Mother
twitching on the lino like dying guppies.
Let's shake this up and change the weather.

Catch! This marvellous drop, like its own tear,
has leaked for years. The tiny Ferris wheel has surfaced
in an oval bubble where it never snows
and little by little all is forgotten. Shhh!
Let's hold the sad toy storms in which we're held,
let's hold them gingerly above the bed,
bubbles gulping contentedly, as we rock them to sleep,
flurries aswim by our gentle skill,
their names on the tips of our tongues.

Allusion

Snowglobes! Is the speaker being disingenuous? He seems to have genuinely forgotten, though his attempt to remember is exactly what creates the poem. And why is he so forgetful? Because he's happy to be, and he's with someone he loves. He explains, but in his own sweet time.

Citizen Kane was something of a myth-kitty for Donaghy. At the beginning of the film, Charles Foster Kane is on his deathbed, looking into his snowglobe; he recalls some snowy childhood idyll . . . and his fat lips part to utter the word 'Rosebud', the name of his childhood sled, and the only thing that ever made him innocently happy. Then he buys the farm, drops the globe, and it smashes. Kane's snowglobe looked much more like a crystal ball, however, hence it *forecasting his past*, which had become as obscure to him as our futures are to us.

This is a sweet, funny and wise poem; it's also a complex one in Donaghy's 'disguised metaphysical' mode, yet he somehow finds plenty of time for sly humour. The Blackpool souvenir is accurately described, and reminds us how surreal and ridiculous these objects really are. *Your mum's souvenir* also establishes that this is not a new relationship. With *see what it says when you turn it over* . . . Donaghy has turned it into a Magic 8-Ball. (These are far more popular in the US – they're a kind of toy oracle in the form of a pool ball filled with clear oil; they have a little window, in which floats a 20-sided die. You ask your question, turn it over, and some nonsense like *it is decidedly so* floats to the surface.) The poet then recalls a hilarious and gruesome Catholic guilt dream, where his own little nativity snowglobe explodes, leaving Mary and Jesus flopping about on the floor, little fish out of their element.

The pun in *This marvellous drop, like its own tear* sends us – with any luck – to Marvell's 'On a Drop of Dew', where the phrase *like its own tear* also occurs. An allusion is an allusion, but this is more than that: it's an intertextual link, and creates a compound sign. Not only does 'Our Life Stories' connect to 'On a Drop of Dew' via quotation, but other aspects of Marvell's poem *also* can now comment on Donaghy's. If we now turn, as instructed, to the Marvell poem, after a beautiful description of the physical dewdrop, the poet makes a symbol out of it:

> So the soul, that drop, that ray
> Of the clear fountain of eternal day,
> (Could it within the human flower be seen,)
> Remembering still its former height,
> Shuns the sweet leaves, and blossoms green,
> And, recollecting its own light,
> Does, in its pure and circling thoughts, express
> The greater heaven in an heaven less.

In this meticulously developed comparison we find a metaphor closely analogous to Donaghy's own. Marvell's dewdrop was no mere dewdrop, but the soul, the little piece of fallen heaven we hold *within the human flower*; similarly, Donaghy's snowglobes are no mere snowglobes, but our defining memories. They are metaphors for the sealed, sentimentally precious episodes by which we constitute our own sense of self. We overrate them. They are *sad toy storms*. And the one he likes best is *leaking* – leaking the amniotic fluid of memory, leaving an empty globe with no bad weather, and nothing we need or can tediously recall. He proposes that lovers, in time, and after the obligatory exchange of *our life stories*, can also perform this blissful amnesiac service for each other, and 'lose themselves' through their lovemaking. The poem ends in an outrageously strange and elaborate image that somehow manages to work, against all the odds. The bed is gently rocking, as love-beds often do, and the silly trinkets are all falling asleep in their little whiteouts, their names on the tips of two tongues that have found a better way to pass the time. Who was it we said we were again?

Pentecost

The neighbours hammered on the walls all night,
Outraged by the noise we made in bed.
Still we kept it up until by first light
We'd said everything that could be said.

Undaunted, we began to mewl and roar
As if desire had stripped itself of words.
Remember when we made those sounds before?
When we built a tower heavenwards
They were our reward for blasphemy.
And then again, two thousand years ago,
We huddled in a room in Galilee
Speaking languages we didn't know,
While amethyst uraeuses of flame
Hissed above us. We recalled the tower
And the tongues. We knew this was the same,
But love had turned the curse into a power.

See? It's something that we've always known:
Though we command the language of desire,
The voice of ecstasy is not our own.
We long to lose ourselves amid the choir
Of the salmon twilight and the mackerel sky,
The very air we take into our lungs,
And the rhododendron's cry.

And when you lick the sweat along my thigh,
Dearest, we renew the gift of tongues.

Tongues

This disarming, funny and sexy poem draws heavily on one of Donaghy's favourite biblical episodes – that cracking bit in Acts 2 when the apostles opened their mouths in the upper room to the assembled multitude, and spoke in tongues of fire:

And when the day of Pentecost was fully come, they were all with one accord in one place. And suddenly there came a sound from heaven as of a rushing mighty wind, and it filled all the house where they were sitting. And there appeared unto them cloven tongues like as of fire, and it sat upon each of them. And they were all filled with the Holy Ghost, and began to speak with other tongues, as the Spirit gave them utterance. And there were dwelling at Jerusalem Jews, devout men, out of every nation under heaven. Now when this was noised abroad, the multitude came together, and were confounded, because that every man heard them speak in his own language. And they were all amazed and marvelled, saying one to another, Behold, are not all these which speak Galileans? And how hear we every man in our own tongue, wherein we were born?

In Charismatic Christianity, the gift of tongues usually arrives with your baptism in the Holy Spirit. You should rightly feel hard done by if it doesn't, given you're just making it all up anyway. The gift of tongues is the ability to speak spontaneously in tongues not your own, just as the apostles did at Pentecost. Conveniently, these can be the tongues of either men *or* angels; wisely, most Christians with the 'gift' tend to claim the latter. (As an ex-Pentecostal, I know angeloglossia to be a whole bunch of mutually incomprehensible dialects. They clearly have a Babel of their own up there.) 'Talking in tongues', then, has come to mean 'talking gibberish and claiming divine inspiration'.

The lovers' inspiration is somewhat less than divine, and *mewl and roar* indicates quite the opposite of an angelic language. Donaghy suggests that this barbaric animal tongue, the tongue of earthly desire, is just what replaced the beautiful ur-language we used to speak before Babel. Before we built the Tower and attempted to storm Heaven by the front door, 'the whole earth was of one language, and of one speech'. God, easily put out at the best of times, was thoroughly miffed: 'Go to, let us go down, and there confound their language, that they may not understand one another's speech.' For a long time this was our best philological explanation for the multiplicity of human tongues, and daft as it is, you have to admit it has a certain neatness. Suddenly we found a thousand low, coarse voices in our heads, and barked and howled like animals, unable to understand one other.

The irony of Pentecost is that it's *almost* the same divine act. God – perhaps a little shamefaced at having to kludge together a fix for his earlier curse, though I wouldn't bet on it – 'confounds' us again, by granting the apostles anti-Babel superpowers. So the curse of mankind's polyglossia is lifted, ironically, by making some men polyglots. But the tongues were strange in the apostolic heads too: their mouths were filled with words they could not understand, and it was, in a sense, Babel all over again. Except *love had turned the curse into a power*.

Amethyst uraeuses of flame / Hissed above us is a wonderful example of Donaghy's favourite 'white noise as a signifier of the beyond' trope, though this one works by sound alone. The line whistles so much, I recall the poet could barely read it without lisping. The highly recherché word *uraeus* is used semi-jocularly.* The poet *knows* no one knows it – but once learned, the image it conjures is extraordinary: it's the hissing snake-symbol on the headgear of Egyptian gods and emperors. *It's something that we've always known*: ecstasy, that which desire seeks out, is *not* desire. It lifts us beyond ourselves, and its tongue is not our own. We speak but don't understand; though who cares, if we're no longer divided from each other? (Another Donaghy trope is his very nuanced used of the first-person plural; as 'we' will see later, it signifies a special, beyond-death indivisibility.)

But then we have a few very strange lines. They're odd enough to make me suspect they're a little *cento*, a collage of quotations, but I've only vague proof. Where do we long to lose ourselves? With *Amid the choir / Of the salmon twilight and the mackerel sky*, he yokes two weather-clichés to mean 'a sensual synaesthetic riot' – but also alludes to one of his touchstone poems, Yeats's 'Sailing to Byzantium'. That poem is also very much taken up with the world that passes, and the world of pure timeless being: '. . . *Those dying generations – at their song, / The salmon-falls, the mackerel-crowded seas.*' As well as Yeats's singing, *Amid the choir* might also nod lightly to the first of Donne's *Funeral Elegies*: *So these high songs that to thee suited bin / Serve but to sound thy Maker's praise and thine, / Which thy dear soul as sweetly sings to him /*

---

* At readings, Donaghy's usual line was 'I'm published by OUP, and we've cut this deal – you may have heard they also do a dictionary, so . . .'

Amid the choir of saints, and seraphim, / As any angel's tongue can sing of thee. The phrase *the very air we take into our lungs* appears in a tract by Ernest Holmes; Holmes was a twentieth-century spiritual author and part of the 'New Thought' movement, which was based on the idea that God is an 'infinite intelligence' and divinity present in us all: *'The breath of Life' is a familiar phrase: let us think of Life as limitless, free and ever-present as the air we breathe. The very air we take into our lungs is the substance of God, charged with the vitalizing power of Divine energy.* As for *rhododendron's cry*, I'm lost. The rhododendron has vaguely erotic overtones in Joyce's *Ulysses*,* but I think it's just supposed to feel like the language is, by now, descending into mad, erotic, synaesthetic glossolalia. (Reading this line, Donaghy would pause just before *cry*, and then lean on it very heavily, in what felt like a spoken wink.) The last two lines, however, are unashamedly raunchy, and tie the conceit together in the most delightfully clear way possible.

The 'excessiveness' of the rude line is emphasized by its being supernumerary to the form: although disguised by its irregular stanzas, the poem is otherwise in perfect rhymed quatrains. This makes the poem twenty-five lines long, which is half fifty; Pentecost means 'fiftieth day' (i.e. after Passover). It takes two to tango. The poem is addressed directly to his dancing partner, though the tone is of careful demonstrative

---

*   They also feature in Derek Mahon's 'A Disused Shed in Co. Wexford', a poem Donaghy greatly admired; the context in which Mahon's flowers appear suggests that he may have been the inspiration here: *What should they do there but desire? / So many days beyond the rhododendrons / With the world waltzing in its bowl of cloud.*

proof. With the odd exception – Barrett Browning and Edna St. Vincent Millay, perhaps – there's been little precedent for this kind of 'formal intimacy' in English poetry since the metaphysical poets. The overall effect is of a hilarious, deliberately affected but also perfectly sincere speech, one that forms an intermezzo between, as they say, 'bouts of lovemaking'. This fact, if no other, identifies it as a young man's poem.

Tears

           are shed, and every day
workers recover
the bloated cadavers
of lovers or lover
who drown in cars this way.

And they crowbar the door
and ordinary stories pour,
furl, crash, and spill downhill –
as water will – not orient,
nor sparkling, but still

Poetic licence

A strange tale, simply told. There is a very short, almost unbearably moving Jack Gilbert poem called 'Games', based on the following proposition: *Imagine if suffering were real . . . Imagine how impossible it would be / to live if some people were / alone and afraid all their lives.* Indeed: imagine if that *were* true? Thank God it isn't. Gilbert and Donaghy never met, to my knowledge, but increasingly, to my mind, they seem kindred spirits – not least because both remain bewilderingly underrated US poets, though at least Gilbert is slowly finding the wide readership he deserves.* Donaghy is the more complex poet of the two, but this poem has a Gilbertesque directness, and asks the same question – *what if suffering were real?* – albeit using a very different rhetorical strategy. Gilbert

---

*   Both Donaghy and Gilbert made the fatal US mistake of being 'hard to pigeonhole'. That we in the UK thought Donaghy one of the greatest US poets when he died was not an opinion frivolously held, but one reached by having carefully read most of the others too. Few readers in the US know of him, even now. Donaghy was flattered to have been taken up by a few of the so-called 'New Formalists' – but equally bewildered by it, as he had little time for either their poetry or theory; the latter he regarded as so much neoconservative bluster, marked by a very superficial understanding of what poetic form was actually *for*. His argument was simply that the old formalists had never gone away; Donaghy improvised wholly within the tradition, and had a very British view of modernism as a strand *of* that longer story, not a break away from it. His essay 'American Revolutions' takes a jaundiced view of the interminable 'raw vs cooked' dialectic in US poetry, and is a boldly unfashionable assault on the long history of Anglophobia in American criticism.

makes his point through ironic inversion; Donaghy, through hyperbole.

In this parallel universe, our crying jags are so productive and prolonged that tears will fill a car. Men are employed by the council to crowbar the drowned from their vehicles, in which they've been lying undiscovered for days; the pressure on the inside is huge, so it's no mean task. When the doors are opened, the waters of their grief take the quickest route to find their level. Finally, water has achieved its aim, to salve, to allay, to lay to rest. Tears will perform this pacific function, eventually, if they're shed in such quantities. The stories that drown us are everyday sorrows: lonelinesses, break-ups, infidelities, rejection. *Lovers or lover* is wonderfully concise; the two alternatives propose very different backstories.

There are light rhymes but one unpaired word, *orient*. This is compensated for by a strong internal chime, *and spill downhill – / as water will*. *Orient* is used here in its seventeenth-century, poetic sense of 'precious like a stone from the Orient, and therefore lustrous, pure and brilliant'. However, its most famous poetic use is probably in Marvell's 'On a Drop of Dew' – *See how the orient dew / Shed from the bosom of the morn / Into the blowing roses*. This poem is heavily alluded to in 'Our Life Stories', where the snowglobe becomes Marvell's dewdrop through the shared phrase 'like its own tear'. I think Donaghy intends to direct us once more to Marvell's self-enclosing, isolated teardrop, and that his making a lonely, unrhymed word of *orient* is quite deliberate. Donaghy's success in adapting a waiter's banal request – 'sparkling or still?' – to such a tragic subject without getting a laugh is a tribute to his remarkable control of tone. Note, too, that the poem pushes off its title so it can begin uncapitalized, and it has no full stop. It can then be read as a continuous circle, hinging on the double sense of 'still': '... *but still / tears / are shed* ...' There's no stopping them, no end to these tears at all.

Timing

Yes I know it's not funny. A prisoner told me
when I was an orderly during the war,
exactly the way that I told it, the whores and the mice.
I say told though I should say he gargled or grunted –
we'd built him a jaw out of one of his ribs
so it took him some time. When he got near the end
and my tunic was freckled with mucus and blood
and the mask of my face ached from grinning
he pulled me down close for the punch line.
He said it. I waited – the way that you waited just now –
but its door never opened.
                              I'm sure that was it,
word for word, though he had neither English nor lips,
because after I searched what remained of his face
he started the torture again. An infection, I reckoned,
and dabbed at his wound and returned to my rounds
but it buzzed round my head like a wasp. Was it code?
If he took me for one of his own in his fever
what might he betray? I ran back at first light
but he'd died in the night of pneumonia.

I'm sure there are those men who laugh out of etiquette,
bafflement, fear of appearing obtuse, or just fear,
and men who dismiss it, or lose it, or change it
before it begins to change them.
Only one in a thousand, perhaps, will remember,
exactly, repeat it, exactly the way that I tell it.
I knew when you hailed me tonight at the station,
I said to myself, as you climbed in the back, he's the one.

Getting it

What's the secret of comedy? It's an old joke, but easy to screw up. The trick is to snap back a badly timed 'Timing!' just after your friend opens their mouth to answer. This poem's joke has also gone awry: it opens after some kind of shaggy dog story has been told by a cabbie to his passenger – a circumstance that isn't revealed until the last two lines, when we realize that we are, literally, a captive audience. *I'd* be laughing nervously. Threes dominate this poem: three characters, three stanzas, and it's in a largely regular triple metre, though the lines vary in their strong stresses between three and five.

What kind of a joke was it, though? Well, it has whores and mice in it. And it wasn't funny. The occasion of its original telling seems even *less* funny. The cabbie was told it by a badly disfigured, jawless prisoner in an unnamed war. We all know the strain of keeping your face fixed in a rictus of grinning anticipation while your uncle tortuously bumbles his way towards a punchline you may or may not understand, or find amusing – but *this* look must have been agony for the speaker to keep up. By the end, our cabbie was covered in spit and blood, and none the wiser: the punchline was impenetrable. Indeed he now thinks it may not have been a joke at all, but an important code that the patient was passing on as a matter of urgency.

Again we see the influence of Borges. What if the 'joke' has to be passed on to one who will understand before the speaker can finally be free of its curse? (It also made me think of Stevenson's short story, *The Bottle Imp* – who confers great riches on anyone who buys it, but whose terrible ultimate curse can only be lifted by selling the bottle – whose contents must be honestly described – at a *lower* price than you bought it for.) And many pretend to have 'gotten it', and laughed anyway, through nervousness or politeness – and then finding they are too distressed by the joke, they've changed it, lost it, tried to put it out of their heads . . . Either way, you've been identified as *the one*. The one in whose mind it will be implanted, word for word, and who can carry the truth of its viral message. And whatever it is, it's no joke.

The Tragedies

Upstage, spotlit, the prince soliloquizes
while courtiers ham their business in the dark.
We see you taking snuff, dim improvisers.
We won't remember, but you've left your mark
within the compass of our sense of sight.

It's how we speed down narrow streets and park.
It's how owls reconnoitre fields by night.

And dimmer, in the wings, the age grows vague
and greyly out of focus. Children die,
a page reports, in papal war and plague.
We glimpse them out the corner of our eye
and see them without looking, without pain.
We aim our minds like arrows at the Dane.

He dies. *Go bid the soldiers shoot*. Applause
like big wings flapping from an autumn field.
Now, as we glance about, the dark withdraws.
The stage dissolves. The orchestra's revealed
as though the light were rising on a tide
past stalls and circle to the streets outside,
as though the vision centred everywhere.

No animal eye can long survive that glare.

> *And let me speak to the yet unknowing world*
> *How these things came about.*

You caught its eye.
Its talons stretched. A silent wing unfurled.
A shadow glided gently from the sky.

Focus

Our waking experience is mostly composed of what's right in front of our noses; but below the limen of conscious processing, we take in a great deal more that drifts in and out of our peripheral vision. We might remember nothing but the great, spotlit speech centre-stage, but all those hammy extras we half-noticed in the wings added something too, even if it was only a little period colour. Yet we navigate by what we see in the corners of our eyes; it's how we quickly reconnoitre an area, how animals search wide fields for signs of movement, and how we spot a parking space. But does this vestigial awareness extend much further than we think? In the play, we're aware of vague reports of great tragedies and enormities in the world beyond, of its slow destruction and decay. The wings extend far beyond those rhubarbing, gesturing bit-parters. Their hints and implications lead us to sketch in whole worlds, whole epochs.

The play is over, and Fortinbras commands a salvo in honour of Hamlet (this arrow-shower echoes our arrow-like focus a couple of lines before). The applause from the audience sounds like wings, bringing to mind that bird of prey mentioned earlier – which we would do well to keep there.* The theatre lights that have kept us fixed on the main act now

---

* A friend points out that Donaghy was much taken up with Van Gogh's *Wheat Field with Crows*, the painting popularly regarded as Vincent's suicide note. I suspect Donaghy also has in mind the panicked scene in the biopic *Lust for Life*, where *Wheat Field* is shown (erroneously) as Vincent's last painting.

rise; we see the whole theatre, the orchestra, the street outside. If the stage's spotlight was equivalent to our focussed and narrowed vision, then this withdrawal of the dark is close to an all-seeing eye. The poet implies that if our conscious minds really suffered such an all-pervading light, we could not survive it. We *require* our focus. But there are other consequences to such a bald light; we have already seen the sinister pun on *wings*, but the clue here is in the double sense of *glare*. (There's no escaping those surveillants in Donaghy's poems, since they're in a win–win situation: the day exposes you, the night hides them.)

Then the poem quotes Horatio, to Fortinbras: *let me tell the world how these terrible things happened*. Here's how: they befell Hamlet because he was singled out by some unseen, terrible dealer of fate. But now the play is over and the focus is no longer on him, the vast, wide light has also exposed *us* . . . And we have had the misfortune to catch the eye of something else, something from above. Tragedy looms, and the *glare* proves fatal. If we should catch the eye of our own doom, it swoops silently upon us like a raptor. If there's any moral here, it's 'keep to the shadows'.

The poem has an odd shape – twenty-six lines, broken into stanzas of five, two, six, seven, one and five lines, but with its rhymes indicating the buried presence of something close to two of Donaghy's thirteen-line 'sonnets'. Once more this reflects his Fibonacci obsessions: while the poem was probably divided this way for purely episodic reasons, the product of $5 \times 2 \times 6 \times 7 \times 1 \times 5$ is 2100, i.e. 21×100, which is neat. At the very least, Donaghy's strong propensity for symbolizing the theme of his poems in their form means that 'twice unlucky' was probably no accident.

Privacy

Here, as in life, they were admitted
to a club exclusive as the Garrick,
now a kind of Victorian Angkor Wat
adjacent to the A road.
Their mossed, sepulchral pieties
neglected for decades, swallowed
back into a mild jungle,
their shapeless sculpture decked
flat, sprayed with uncouth rhymes,
violated by ritual necrophilia in the 60s,
how fares it with the happy dead?

The PM urges their revival,
the spirits of industry, exploration,
eels and gin, the floorless jig.
Here, everyone knows his place.
Here, little green bronze bells
festoon the exterior of the 'Egyptian' mausoleum.
The strings once led inside,
where, waking in their two inch dark,
the prematurely interred
could tintinnabulate as if for tea.
Sadly, these have snapped.

Class

This is a private cemetery. Which is ridiculous, when you think about it; and the poet asks that we do just that. Death is the great leveller, yet this place insists that a better class of dead awaits in First. Donaghy compares this gentleman's club of the existentially disadvantaged to the great twelfth-century Cambodian temple complex of Angkor Wat: both were grandiose conceptions which fell into jungled ruin. It turns out no one really cares much for the welfare of the long dead, nor the upkeep of their baroque and silent cities.

Donaghy nods cynically towards Gray's 'Elegy Written in a Country Churchyard', stealing several of its phrases – *Yet even these bones from insult to protect / Some frail memorial still erected nigh, / With uncouth rhymes and shapeless sculpture decked, / Implores the passing tribute of a sigh* . . . except Gray found the *uncouth rhymes* and *shapeless sculpture* of his rustic cemetery rather moving. *Decked* here is reappropriated as the verb 'to flatten', as in 'to lay out with a punch'; *uncouth rhymes* aren't crude-but-heartfelt epitaphs, but those of spray-can graffitists. It looks like these dead have also been sexually assaulted by drug-crazed hippies. Excellent . . . Then he quotes, with wonderful sarcasm, a passage from Tennyson's *In Memoriam* (where the poet goes on to ask if, in the lovely eternal amnesia of heaven, his beloved Arthur Hallam ever spares him half a thought): *How fares it with the happy dead?* The answer is clearly 'not so great'.

What does it then mean to say the PM is calling for the *revival* of these *spirits*? A call for the good old days, a Britain where everyone *knows their place*?* The time of great industrialists and explorers, eel pie and mash, mother's ruin. The 'floorless jig' was a grim little metaphor for the dance performed by a hanging man, and so is here used as a metonym for 'bringing back capital punishment'.

And here they lie, in their exclusive, sequestered part of the cemetery, cemented in their station. The upper classes were rarely comfortable with the prospect of their own non-immortality, and many were terrified of live burial – though not without reason. By present standards, Victorian brain-death was somewhat laxly defined; there were a number of well-reported cases of premature interment, where, in the process of reopening the grave to accommodate new family members, it was revealed that Mum had not died serenely at home in her sleep but clawing off her fingernails underground.† If they happened to wake in the *two inch dark* (i.e. between your nose and the coffin lid, another terrifying

---

* I suspect Donaghy has in mind the infamous Tory 'Back to Basics' campaign of the 1990s. Rather wonderfully, 'Back to Basics' – a clarion call for a return to the good old family values of clean living, decency and mutual respect – almost immediately became synonymous with certain other old-fashioned values, i.e. the same sleaze and corruption that always goes hand-in-hand with power and gross economic disparity. At least the Victorians knew how to keep it out of the press.

† Donaghy insisted that he would not be buried, and I think he had such horrors in mind. I once asked him how he'd prefer to be disposed of; he said 'liquidized'. Maddy Paxman asked him the same question, and Spike replied that he'd like to be stuffed like Jeremy Bentham, then returned to his armchair with his coffee cup, since no one would notice the difference. Coffee once almost killed him: the Donaghy ristretto consisted of a whole bag of Italian roast dumped in a cafetière, then downed in one.

metonym) it was fine: their preposterous mausoleums also had an underground system of pulleys and wires leading to little bells that could be rung at the surface. 'Sorry to be a bore old chap – not quite dead yet.' Alas, the class system has not been maintained very carefully, and all has fallen into disrepair – oops – the result being rather more 'privacy' than they'd calculated for. The morals of this poem are simply a) be careful what you wish for, and b) you can have too much of a good thing.

Incidentally, the fenced-off necropolis described here lies within Highgate cemetery, where Donaghy once applied for the job of tour guide. He failed the interview. Given his propensity for making stuff up, this was probably just as well. Donaghy's ashes are buried there, below a memorial plaque bearing a line from 'The Present'.

Ramon Fernandez?

I met him when I fought in the brigade,
In Barcelona, when the people had it.

Red flags snapped above the tower clock
Of what had been renamed the 'Lenin Barracks'.
The ancient face was permanently fixed,
If memory serves, at half eleven.
Dead right twice a day.

Fernandez played guitar each day at noon
In the plaza beneath the barracks tower,
Hawking his revolutionary broadsides.
And as he sang he stared up at the clock
As if he half expected it to move.

I recall the way he played the crowd
Sure as he played his lacquered blue guitar.
I recall the troop trains pulling from the station,
White knuckles over carbines, boys' voices
Singing the anthems of Ramon Fernandez.

And I wonder if anyone caught on but me.
The songs the fascists sang across the wire
Were his, the same he sang, got us to sing.
A few words changed, not many. *Libertad*,
Hermana Libre, I have them all by heart.

One day he vanished back across the front
And later, when the town was under siege,
A stray round hit the barracks clock and cracked
Both iron hands clean off but left the face
To glare like a phase of the moon above the burning city.

Art

This is a good example of the kind of Donaghy poem one can skate over or plunge into. The fact that you can choose between those readings – and that both can return consistent, if rather different experiences – shows to what degree his poetry possessed the underrated virtue of 'optional depth'. Read straight, this is a witty account of a sloganeer who works for both sides, but it also says something profound about the troubled relationship between art and politics, and the unreliability of the artist.

Ramon *who*? It's a long story. If you know this guy at all, it's likely from Wallace Stevens's 'The Idea of Order at Key West'. Insofar as one of the key poems of the modernist movement is amenable to paraphrase: Stevens uses the image of a woman singing of the sea (and to, with, about and *as* the sea) to address the way that we receive the materials of the world to make art, and in doing so become artificers of the world ourselves. But even after the singing, after the art has stopped – the *ideas of order* we have visited on the world still obtain, and our way of beholding it has been fundamentally changed. Ramon Fernandez turns up late in the poem:

> Ramon Fernandez, tell me, if you know,
> Why, when the singing ended and we turned
> Toward the town, tell why the glassy lights,
> The lights in the fishing boats at anchor there,
> As night descended, tilting in the air,
> Mastered the night and portioned out the sea,
> Fixing emblazoned zones and fiery poles,
> Arranging, deepening, enchanting night.

Stevens claimed that since the poem was a fiction, the name of his companion was pulled out of the hat. I suspect this was disingenuous: he will have been aware of the Mexican-born French critic of the same name from *The Dial*, the literary magazine where they had both published. This Ramon Fernandez is now more famous for one of the strangest political journeys ever made by a Western intellectual. In the words of his son, the French novelist Dominique Fernandez: 'I try to explain to myself . . . how this man, one of the most brilliant intellectuals of his age, could be a socialist at the age of 31, the literary critic of a leftist newspaper at 38, a Communist at 40, a Fascist at 43, and finally collaborationist at 46.' It was this final move which won him his lasting notoriety. As a member of the French Fascist Party, Fernandez became an enthusiastic collaborator after France fell to the Nazis in 1940. Fernandez was born in 1894; in 1934, the date of his poem's composition, Stevens will have known him as a communist or leftist – but one who had become so while actively resisting the clean solutions of fascism. Fernandez had published a widely circulated essay called 'I Came Near Being a Fascist' in the *Partisan Review*, in which he rejected the self-interested right-wing radicalization of the French intellectual class. Stevens may or may not have been familiar with the piece, but given that he was trying to establish his own anti-fascist credentials at the time, the choice of Ramon Fernandez as his fictional companion may not have been entirely accidental.

Sean O'Brien has proposed a subtler reason:

> With his public announcements of political commitments and conversions, Fernandez was the opposite of Stevens, who recoiled at the idea of associating himself with any

group or programme that offered 'solutions'. Fernandez, suggests Stevens in 'The Idea of Order', might have been certain about the source and effect of the singer's song, but the only thing Stevens was sure of was that in his certainty, Fernandez would have been wrong.

Taking both points together, however, might explain both Stevens's choice of companion in the poem, *and* his interrogation of him.

Donaghy will have been aware of both Ramons, and both inform this third Ramon. Here, he's the man who played for both sides – but he's also Stevens's friend: he is, as it turns out, 'The Man With the Blue Guitar' – another key Stevens poem that deals with the imagination's power to transform external reality. *Things as they are / Are changed upon the blue guitar.* Certainly in the way *he played the crowd* Ramon seemed to regard reality as something to be manipulated, and – like the real-world Ramon – political allegiance as a something you might change like your shirt. The title both proposes a question the poem will answer: *You're asking who this guy was? Let me tell you . . .* and attaches a question mark to Fernandez's name, as if it were part of it.

The speaker in the poem is fighting for the International Brigade in the Spanish Civil War. We might also guess that he could be Irish – in which case the *blue* of Ramon's guitar will have had a further resonance. The Irish National Guard, the 'Blueshirts', were not quite out-and-out fascists – but they were fiercely anti-communist, and in some ways saw their work as equivalent to that of the Italian Blackshirts. A number of the Blueshirts fought for Franco in the Civil War (Donaghy's uncle in 'Auto da Fé' was likely among them). For the speaker, they would have represented a cohort *worse* than the enemy.

The poem is set *in Barcelona, when the people had it*. The action takes place near the communist stronghold of 'The Lenin Barracks'. (There were 'Karl Marx Barracks' and 'Bakunin Barracks' too; Claude Simon has uncomfortably claimed – contradicting Orwell's account of Barcelona in 1936 as some kind of proletarian idyll – that the factions gathered round each barracks were defined by mutual loathing, and that they all regarded each other as counter-revolutionaries.) Here, Ramon would play his guitar at noon in the plaza, singing and peddling his rousing songs of the revolution. The clock, like all stopped clocks, was right twice a day. The dead clock turns out to be Ramon's 'symbolic correlative' here: he also times his daily appearances carefully, and changes barely a word of his songs, which are 'right twice' in both camps. Because of this, I think his glance to the clock is a nervous one: if *it* moves, he'll be revealed as a traitor, a double agent, an amoral opportunist. (Seeing 11.30, Ramon will feel he has turned up half an hour early; he's a man ahead of his time. I'm not sure of the significance of this hour, though it will likely have one. There are about as many arbitrary details in Donaghy as there are in Donne, Borges, Bishop or Muldoon, i.e. almost none.)

The speaker now imparts the killer detail. He has discovered that *both* sides sing the songs of Ramon Fernandez – both the terrified young troops leaving the station, and the fascists over the dividing wire. *Freedom, free sister . . .* Then *One day he vanished back across the front*. The word *back* suggests that Ramon was indeed a mole, a spy. When the city is besieged, the clock comes under attack. You'll recall Ramon's earlier problems with that clock; I wonder if he *himself* has wiped its face – I'm not sure I quite believe it was *a stray round*. He has no need of pretence, now, and can be right *no* times a day. If we give this poem a more intertextual reading, and place it within the context of the Stevens poem to which it's carefully linked: with 'the singing ended' and Ramon gone, there *are* no longer 'ideas of order'. The clock face may now be empty, but the moon's 'phase' is full. This is the moon of lunacy, sleeplessness and the hunt, and it glares in active surveillance while the city burns beneath it, and falls into bloody chaos.

Donaghy is telling us that art and order do *not* go hand in hand, and our occasional elevation of the artist to the status of an angel of order and harmony is a sentimentalism. They are often unaligned, self-interested manipulators, and are just as capable of being agents of total disorder and mayhem.*

---

* This particular poem was, incidentally, dismissed by Roy Hattersley as 'trite' when he sat on the panel of the Whitbread Prize. I gather that Donaghy might have otherwise been up for the overall book of the year for *Shibboleth*.

Reliquary

The robot camera enters the *Titanic*
And we see her fish-cold nurseries on the news;
The toys of Pompeii trampled in the panic;
The death camp barrel of babyshoes;

The snow that covered up the lost girl's tracks;
The scapular she wore about her neck;
The broken doll the photojournalist packs
to toss into the foreground of the wreck.

Evidence

A *reliquary*, the small box or casket in which saintly relics are kept, is a repository of metonyms. The difference between the reliquaries of the faithful and the little reliquary of this poem is that saintly relics are nonsense – or at least they were certainly believed to be by the author. This box of genuine horrors is very far removed from the fake, sentimental tokens we keep locked in gilded caskets in our cathedrals. However, the poem does address the question of how important the authenticity of the facts really are.

A relic is kept as a remembrance or souvenir of a person, event or place. Its etymology is a 'leaving', i.e. 'that which remains'. The robot camera is a dead, disinterested all-seeing eye which provides the photomontage of the whole poem, not just the initial image of the sunken *Titanic*, of which it is a part. All six items in this grim eight-liner are tokens of that very worst thing, the stolen childhood; they are the relics of dead children. The first stanza consists of three jump-cut images from newsreels: the drowned boat, the lava-buried city, the gas chambers and their haul of little shoes. They have an elemental feel: death by water, by fire, by air . . . For this reason I hear a shallow grave implied in *the lost girl*. The girl's scapular has, it seems, been found. This returns us to the religious theme of the title. A nun's scapular is something different, but here it's a devotional object which consists of two squares of cloth or paper bearing biblical images or texts, joined by two bands of material. It's very unlikely to have been merely abandoned, and therefore works as an ironic symbol, since the scapular is supposed to offer the Virgin's protection. (Who *is* this girl? She seems important. I've been unable to establish her identity, though I feel the poet has someone specific in mind.)

We are told to read these tokens just like those of the saints: fetishized, horrifically treasurable, the morbid relics of our anti-miracles. The poet seems to suggest that the cynicism of the journalist – who brings along a broken doll for no purpose but to bolster the emotional punch of their photo of some unnamed catastrophe – may be neither here nor there: it is the final item in a list of otherwise authentic images. Perhaps these earlier images were 'doctored' too, even if only in the manner of their effective presentation? The truth is that the last line problematizes the matter in a way that destabilizes the entire poem: Donaghy 'detested cheap sentiment', and perhaps the poem is also about how little we can trust our own responses, given how quick others are to manipulate them. For me, what's true is our *feeling* about real events – and whatever prompts that real feeling will suffice, whether the means are authentic or not. The saints may be fake, and their relics even more so. The doll is fake too. But the children are real, and dead.

The River in Spate

                 sweeps us both down its cold grey current.
Grey now as your father was when I met you,
I wake even now on that shore where once,
sweat-slick and still, we breathed together –
in – soft rain gentling the level of the lake,
out – bright mist rising from the lake at dawn.
How long before we gave each other to sleep,
to air – drawing the mist up, exhaling the rain?
Though we fight now for breath and weaken
in the torrent's surge to the dark of its mouth,
you are still asleep in my arms by its source,
small waves lapping the gravel shore,
and I am still awake and watching you,
in wonder, without sadness, like a child.

Quiet

This is a loose unrhymed sonnet with a roughly i.p. line-length that varies considerably. It's an undervalued poem of Donaghy's – mainly, I think, because its language is so quiet, and its conceit old and familiar: time is a relentless river, bearing us helplessly to the sea. (*Oh lad, I fear that yon's the sea / Where they fished for you and me, / And there, from whence we both were ta'en, / You and I shall drown again . . .* Housman, 'The West'.) But the best conceits are infinitely serviceable. That we repeatedly identify such a strong common motif in the flow of time and of water surely tells us something about the basic motifs on which the universe improvises.

This very Shakespearian poem is about love, and how it works as a stay against that inexorable current. (I don't know to what extent Donaghy wanted us to connect these lines with a fairly well-known early poem of Louis MacNeice's, 'River in Spate'; they share a death-theme, but Donaghy's is focussed on the source, not the torrent.) Here, time pulls the lovers faster and faster towards the river's dark mouth; but there's something in us that resists this natural law, something in the function of memory that triumphs over it. The poet looks back to a blissful time in early love, by the lake shore. Then, the lovers were at one with the apparently stationary nature of time itself; their breathing was at one with the cyclical renewal of the world – breathing down and in the rain, breathing out and up the mist that will condense to fall again. Perhaps they did not even *know* that the lake was the source of the river; it was too continuous with their still selves to suspect as much. What was their mistake? Falling *asleep*; not remaining wakefully attentive to one another, as love demands. Here, this has the effect of inverting the perfectly balanced weather-cycle the poet had described. They give themselves up not just to sleep – but, in sleep's disembodied state, *to air*; they are now *above* the lake, breathing down the rain that will soon tip the scales, bring the flood, then the current strong enough to sweep them away.

If we cease in our wakeful attention, the poem says, we fall. We fall from the eternal moment to our time-driven lives, fall into that river that takes us, all too soon, back to the sea again. (We're obliged to observe that the woman has fallen asleep first; which is to say there's a buried or unconscious note of accusation here.) But even as they roar and rush to their cold grey end, there is still something in their love that's more than mere comfort. Their lovers' idyll is somewhere intact, and as real as the day they first entered it. What was experienced as eternal must, by definition, remain eternal.

Southwesternmost

I've a pocketwatch for telling space,
a compass tooled for reckoning by time,
to search this quadrant between six and nine
for traces of her song, her scent, her face.
Come night, that we might seek her there, come soon,
come shade the southwest quarter of this chart,
the damaged chamber of my mother's heart.

Mare Serenitatis on the moon,
this blindspot, tearhaze, cinder in the eye,
this cloudy star when I look left and down,
this corner of the crest without a crown,
this treeless plain where she went home to die.
I almost hear it now and hold its shape,
the famine song she's humming in my sleep.

Difficulty and interpretation

This odd sonnet is broken into two equal seven-line stanzas, but nonetheless honours an English rhyme scheme of ABBA CDDC EFFE GG. It's in fairly fluent and regular i.p., at least if you can admit the first line by accenting 'I've' (which the author did, when he read it aloud). Its beautiful riddle is not fully comprehensible to me, and I sense rather than understand the unity it makes. In some ways it just seems a riff on the vague category of 'the southwesternmost', in what appears to be a kind of elegy for the poet's mother: she was a Kerrywoman, and Co. Kerry is the southwesternmost part of Ireland. The title declares the theme honestly enough, I think, and suggests we might interrogate the word in several ways – the directional, the geographic, the navigational. But the poet means more than this – almost a 'southwesternmostness' of the spirit. With *I've a pocketwatch for telling space, / a compass tooled for reckoning by time* – he introduces two impossible, magical devices, with which we might navigate through space-time to this strange lower-left-hand quarter of the soul. We might raise the dead through such machines. We need it to be night for them to work, though, since dark provides the only light we can steer by here. What is it we need night to see? The moon, the stars; the things that appear to us in dreams; the ghosts of the dead. *This chart* is the poem's own spatiotemporal, synaesthetic map: an astrological natal chart or a navigational chart seems unlikely. The beautiful line *the damaged chamber of my mother's heart* I assume refers to his mother's left ventricle, as well as her inability, perhaps, to express or give certain kinds of love. (The repeated affricate sounds of 'damaged chamber' and the phrase's double half-assonance give it great lyric force.) This seems to give the riddle away: the poem is an elegy of sorts.*

Of the list in the second stanza of 'bright things seen better in the dark', *Mare Serenitatis on the moon* is in some ways the most confusing line, since viewed from most northern cities – certainly New York, Kerry, Chicago or London – the Sea of Serenity is roughly central nor'nor'east in the moon's circle.† I think he's probably just referring to the ragged shape of the crater – also a symbol, in this poem, of cold, remote serenity, and a peace alike unto death. Clues to a sensible interpretation lie in recordings of Donaghy in performance; reading this poem, he would place a rising accent on 'moon' in a kind of 'performed colon', followed by a deaccent on the word 'this' immediately before 'blindspot' – which is what you do when you either demote something to grammatical function, or elide

---

* I learn from Maddy Paxman's memoir, *The Great Below*, that before she died Donaghy's mother had a replacement valve fitted, the noise from which caused her great distress.

† Mare Humorum, 'the sea of moisture', is SSW in the moon's compass, seen from the northern hemisphere. Only in Australia would Mare Serenitatis be SW. If we look in the southwestern corner of the sea itself, we find Sulpicius gallus, a crater named for the great Roman general and orator Gaius Sulpicius Gallus, who was most famous for predicting an eclipse of the moon on the night before the Battle of Pydna in 168 BC. He later devoted himself to astronomy. During the *Apollo 17* module orbits in 1972, Harrison Schmitt noted the red-orange splashes of coloured volcanic glass in the walls of some craters nearby, and . . . No! Enough! I include this only to show what can happen if you go barking up the wrong tree. The trouble is that there are many occasions where a Donaghy line deliberately invites just such paranoid scrutiny.

it. This leads me to believe his intention might be *Mare Serenitatis on the moon* – [yes, in summary, that's what this list of things is: *this*] *blindspot, tearhaze, cinder in the eye . . .*

Blindspot, tearhaze, cinder in the eye also form a list of various southwestern occlusions: by self-blindness, by emotion or sentimentality, by misadventure – and then by what sounds like the author's macular degeneration with *this cloudy star when I look left and down*. If this is *literally* the case, the author sounds like he has macular oedema, which I'd be paying more attention to than his worries over inheriting his mother's heart condition.*

As for the empty quadrant of *this corner of the crest without a crown*, I suspect it refers to the southwest quadrant of the crest of the British Isles: the Harp of Eire, which is the British Isles' only crownless republic; it's a lovely, context-appropriate metonym for Ireland. As for *the treeless plain* – Kerry is treeless, but I don't think she went there to die, other than in her own mind. Either way, the bleakness is plain enough. Enough, certainly, to summon the shape of the bleak song she's humming to the author, as a lullaby. (At this point all I can hear in my head is the almost unbearable melancholy of Busoni's *Berceuse Élégiaque*, his coffin-lullaby for his dead mother.)

In Scotland, we think of the famine song as a wretched little number sung by half-witted Rangers supporters to half-witted Celtic supporters (sectarian tension is almost

---

* I know too much of this stuff, and so did Donaghy, for the same reasons. Donaghy, incidentally, was obsessed with his cardiac arrhythmia; ironically, it turned out that he had the heart of an Irish ox, which the doctors had a hard time actually getting to stop after the machines were switched off.

unknown in Scotland *except* for Glasgow, where it mimics that of Belfast, to the bewildered boredom of the rest of the country). 'If we hadn't have taken them in / Fed them and washed them / Thousands in Glasgow alone / From Ireland they came / Brought us nothing but trouble and shame / Well the famine is over / Why don't they go home?' This isn't that one, though; the famine song has older precedents. One more likely candidate runs:

> Oh, the praties they grow small over here,
> Oh, the praties they grow small over here,
> Oh, the praties they grow small, and we dig them in the fall
> And we eat them, skin and all, over here
>
> Oh, we're down into the dust, over here,
> Oh, we're down into the dust, over here,
> Oh, we're down into the dust, but the Lord in whom we trust
> Will repay us crumb for crust over here.

In poetry, the more strange or disturbing the thing we have to say, the more beautifully we tend to sing it: music tricks the brain into briefly entertaining the unthinkable – the logically impossible, nonsensical, strange or alien statement that it would otherwise instinctively reject. The lyric weave of this strange poem is especially rich. If we take a passage at random: *this blindspot, tearhaze, cinder in the eye, / this cloudy star when I look left and down, / this corner of the crest without a crown . . .* we find it tightly held together by its sibilance, and the unvoiced guttural and dental sounds of [k] and [t]; in the next line, 'plain' echoes 'blind' and 'treeless' echoes 'tear haze', creating, via their shared sounds, vague, sad, empty compound signs in the back of the reader's mind. (Because we process poetry as half-song, we allow sound to conduct sense through a kind of phonetic metaphor.) Either way, the poem does its work in darkness but sings as clear as day, even if its meaning is sometimes obscure – or as here, clouded by its own sad dream.

The apparatus

What was that exquisite name,
Could I but reach and touch it?
    The hand arranging beads across
Her cold hand in the casket.

Where is that gentle token
By which I tell my love?
    This unopened envelope,
This single empty glove.

She was my lover when we met
How could I betray her?
    The stillness in the photograph
Of a raging river.

Where are the tools by which I map
These planetary motions?
    They come and go beyond your reach.
They make their own decisions.

Who is my accuser?
Who keeps watch all afternoon?
    A glass eye, in a locked drawer,
In a forgotten room.

Self-impersonation

Donaghy's last collection, *Safest*, contains around ten of his finest poems. As a whole, though, it's more of a mixed bag – inevitably, the book was left unfinished. However, a few poems seem to point to a shift in his work that 'had he lived' (I can't say this with much conviction) might have opened up a new seam. 'The apparatus' *appears* to be one such; stylistically, there's little else quite like it in Donaghy's oeuvre. However, I think this would amount to an optimistic misreading. 'The apparatus' is a dead end, but almost a self-consciously deliberate one. It's a fine poem – but *not*, paradoxically, when read in the context of his work as a whole, within which it diminishes to something like self-parody.

'The apparatus' is Donaghy's 'Song of Myself', and it is a grievously sad one. (Mercifully, he was not an individual entirely taken up with himself.) It's written in ballad form with a few minor variations, and consists of a series of questions, each answered obliquely. However, if we look at what those fretful queries actually address, we find little but Donaghy's perennial obsessions, which are listed so diligently the poem is almost an act of knowing self-caricature. And that may have been his intention; he was, I believe, finishing his work, and in such states of mind we tend towards the summary. The apparatus, the structure that drove and supported his research in this life, was as follows: the loss of something precious from the memory, and memory as something death will divide us from; the one-sided, hollow, self-reflexive and unstable nature of love; the persistence of a motionless eternal within the raging flow of time; the relinquishing of control and volition to the paradoxes of fate and to a deterministic universe; and paranoia, guilt and surveillance. Like 'Disquietude', there isn't a single line in this poem which does not recall another Donaghy had already written, but here – as Randall Jarrell said of the later Auden – he's become himself to the nth degree. The man sounds so very tired of it all.

The Swear Box

They open, at forty, cabinets their fathers locked,
boys again, whispering bad words beneath blankets,
girls spitting the big verbs at their mirrors.
Something sharp and rusty on their tongues again,
something more he'd hoped to spare them:
new bedside silences for visiting hours,
new definitions for never, for over,
quiet words boomed from pulpit mics,
and, afterwards, the whispers of dark-suited cousins.
Women hugging pregnant friends practice
new phrases, concealing the chill. Grown men
yank shut the curtains of their brilliant studies
to stop the black glass listening.

Swearing

This is a late poem, and a dark one. It's an 'unlucky sonnet' of thirteen lines (yes, it's the Fibonacci thing again) that feels very extempore for Donaghy: there isn't the usual, almost-deranged integration of parts that we generally find in his work, but it's a powerful poem nonetheless. It addresses the mid-life condition its author was, I suspect, partly relieved to put behind him. Although it makes no great difference whether the reader realizes or not, this poem takes its cue from a well-known chiller by Donald Justice called 'Men at Forty': *Men at forty / Learn to close softly / The doors to rooms they will not be / Coming back to.* That poem also concerns fathers: *And deep in mirrors / They rediscover / The face of the boy as he practices tying / His father's tie there in secret / And the face of that father . . .*

Our options might be dwindling, and one door closing while another slams shut – but something *else* has swung open, after being locked for so long. The Swear Box. Not where you'd place a coin as penance when you said a bad word, but a box *full* of bad words you were once forbidden to speak. A box of swearing, and for swearing inside.

When we first road-tested those words alone, or declined the verb *to fuck* before a mirror, it was for the dangerous, grown-up thrill on our tongues. But now we swear through necessity. Now, in the terrible hospital silences, armed with the knowledge of what it *really* means for things to be done, over, impossible, lost – the recreational cursing begins again. We curse at terminal illness, lost hope, divorce, the betrayal of friends. We swear at the deaths of family members, redundancy, childlessness. We naturally tend to hear the word 'new' as a positive and optimistic word; here, its hammered initial repetition reminds us that it need not be. In the four consecutive strong stresses of *grown men yank shut* I can hear a terrorized urgency, and see the poet standing in his over-lit, scared-of-the-dark room (hence *grown men*), a room full of his useless, book-lined 'brilliance' – the acquired knowledge that has served no purpose, brought no enlightenment or comfort, and offered no real protection. (*Black glass* is a Heaneyesque touch: one monosyllable qualified by a second, the phrase made salient by its bold assonance and unified by its near-palindromic consonantal pattern.) He pulls his curtains shut against the endless surveillance of the night, that listening darkness – one thinks of the priest in 'Confessions' – that will judge him for his sin. *Fuck. Fuck. Fuck.*

Two Spells for Sleeping

Eight white stones
in a moonlit garden,
to carry her safe
across the bracken
on a gravel path
like a silvery ribbon
seven eels in the urge of water
a necklace in rhyme
to help her remember
a river to carry her
unheard laughter
to light about her
weary mirror
six candles for a king's daughter
five sighs for a drooping head
a prayer to be whispered
a book to be read
four ghosts to gentle her bed
three owls in the dusk falling
what is that name
you hear them calling?
In the soft dark welling,
two tales to be telling,
one spell for sleeping,
one for kissing,
for leaving.

Spells

A spell should do its work by invisible means. If you understand it, you ruin the very mystery on which its efficacy depends. This poem was originally commissioned as a poem for children, but personally I wouldn't let any child near it. As beautiful as it is, I'm not convinced its double charm is age-appropriate, or that any child who heard it would necessarily wake up again; its title suggests that things might go either way. (The poem put me strongly in mind of Chuck Palahniuk's notorious horror story *Lullaby*, where an unexplained outbreak of Sudden Infant Death Syndrome is traced to a children's anthology, *Poems and Rhymes around the World*, in which an African 'culling song' had been inadvertently gathered.) Its feel of finality seemed unequivocal enough for us to place it last in *Safest* – the book we compiled after Donaghy's death – though this may have overstated its note of personal leave-taking. I'm being cautious, because I can't figure this poem out at all. It's easy to fall under the spell of its music, and ignore its strangeness, its syntactic oddness, its hints of a buried narrative or secret sequence. I very much doubt it's merely the list of casually associative, quietly suggestive images that it appears. Maddy Paxman has rightly pointed out to me that there's something of Christina Rossetti about this – perhaps he had 'Holy Innocents' or 'Dream Land' in his head when he wrote it.

Since it's a counting-song, or rather a countdown, numbers will probably offer at least some of the key. Twenty-six lines make twice thirteen, the most mysterious number in charms, cures and curses, as all Fibonacci addicts (amongst which

Michael reigned supreme, and yes, I know I've said this thirteen times) know only too well. Removing the non-Fibonacci numbers and the lines which follow them leaves a smoother result – but that doesn't seem the answer. Nor does reading alternate lines, reading it backwards, or any more complex pattern I can think of. Nor does any interrogation of its image-sequence: eight stones; seven eels; six candles; five sighs; four ghosts; three owls; two tales; one double spell . . . Other than its vague progression from the material to the immaterial. (*Owls* make a kind of sense in this organizing principle, since they are almost universally considered bad omens.) Then it occurred to me that I've spent so long trying to plumb the mysteries of this peculiar, lovely, fretful song . . . I've done nothing but repeat it over, and over, and over again. Was that the real reason he sowed the intrigue? Either way, I'm feeling sleepy, and I'm going to stop here.

Upon a Claude Glass

A lady might pretend to fix her face,
but scan the room inside her compact mirror –

so gentlemen would scrutinize this glass
to gaze on Windermere or Rydal Water

and pick their way along the clifftop tracks
intent upon the romance in the box,

keeping unframed nature at their backs,
and some would come to grief upon the rocks.

Don't look so smug. Don't think you're any safer
as you blunder forward through your years

squinting to recall some fading pleasure,
or blinded by some private scrim of tears.

I know. My world's encircled by this prop,
though all my life I've tried to force it shut

Symbol

Sometimes we stumble upon a new symbol whose truth and perfection we immediately recognize. Were one to set about writing a poem about our wretched habit of living half our lives in the bitter or sentimentalized past, it would be hard to think of a better metaphor than that of the Claude Glass. Indeed, it fits so well that I think it's very likely that symbol prompted the poem, not vice versa. The trouble is that few of us now know what a Claude glass is – but the poet takes advantage of our ignorance, and takes the opportunity to offer an explanation through which the power of his symbol becomes clear.

Named after the French landscape painter Claude Lorrain, the Claude glass was a tinted, convex hand-mirror which artistic and sensitive types would take with them on nature rambles. Held before you and slightly to one side, it had the effect of converting the landscape behind into a miniature, picturesque scene, supposedly reminiscent of the soft, darkened gradations of Lorrain's work. In the early Romantic era it was popular with Sunday painters and visitors to the wilder parts of rural England in the first days of inland tourism. Unsurprisingly, the practice of fell-walking while looking backwards in a mirror occasionally proved fatal; as the bodies mounted, so did the derision, and mercifully the glass was soon forgotten.

This i.p. sonnet in couplets is a chirpy and straightforward affair for the octave, which merely describes the device – but at the turn, the tone changes. *Don't look so smug.* We're just as ridiculous. We blunder ahead while blinded by our forever backwards-looking minds, our thoughts tinted, tainted and soured by memory, or blurred by teary sentimentality. We too will die by our perverse determination to ignore what's right in front of us. The author's world, too, is similarly circumscribed: there's no full stop at the end of the poem, no closure, and only a half rhyme – this wretched mirror *will not close*, and stays jammed open. How many of us ever dare to turn round, and really face the *unframed nature* of our own being here?

For the most part, this little book avoids too much tech-talk; I think that stuff is rarely of much interest or relevance to the general reader. However, the relative simplicity of this funny and grim poem leaves me a little space to talk about the phenomenon of intonational stress – which *is* matter for the reader's concern, so bear with me. When Donaghy read this poem, certain words would receive an intonational accent or deaccent for emphasis or de-emphasis. What such a performance supplies is a whole layer of additional phonological information which encodes a great deal of semantic and emotional sense. Words supply broad meaning, but it's the musical line of our performance that tells others what we mean *by* those words. Alas, faced with just the page, we have nothing but our sensitivity, good taste and intelligence with which to recreate these accents. For many poems, we can get by on this; but the more subtle, complex or difficult the poem, the more a well-placed intonational rise or fall will help identify the most important piece of information in the phrase, or the one the poet thinks you should already know, or realize an ironic tone, or distinguish between a genuine and a rhetorical question, and so on. Because poetry will often try to cram a huge amount of information into a few lines, all these semantic space-saving dimensions can be terrifically important. We have a denotative layer of uppermost sense, but also (to name a few of them) a connotative layer, an allusive layer, a prosodic layer, an allegorical layer . . . and a performative layer of phonological contour, or, if you like, a performed 'song'. Getting it onto the page is a problem poetry has never got to grips with, alas, and most attempts at typographical solutions have been ugly or confusing. For the record, though, Donaghy would read it with the following intonational rises:

> A lady might *pretend* to fix her face,
> but scan the *room* inside her compact mirror –
>
> so gentlemen would scrutinize *this* glass
> to gaze on *Windermere* or Rydal Water
>
> and *pick* their way along the clifftop tracks
> intent upon the romance in the box,
>
> keeping *unframed* nature at their backs,
> and *some* would come to grief upon the rocks.
>
> Don't look so smug. Don't think you're any *safer*
> as you blunder forward through your years
>
> squinting to recall some *fading* pleasure,
> or blinded by some private scrim of tears.
>
> *I* know. *My* world's encircled by this prop,
> though *all my life* I've *tried* to *force* it *shut*

I'm simplifying, and brutally; there was far more information in his voice than I can convey using only crude italics, but this isn't a phonology lecture. Nonetheless, this can tell us quite a lot. Most of the emphases are contrastive, and they just make salient the most important new fact in the phrase.

Some, though, are subtler: '*pick* their way' and '*fading* pleasure' are delivered with a delicious light sarcasm, in full knowledge of their own tired, sentimental collocations; the last line 'though *all my life* I've *tried* to *force* it *shut*' enacts the physical struggle of closing this clam from hell, and so on. All of which poses an interesting question: if the poet is dead, and has made no recording of it – is there a dimension of the poem potentially lost for ever? Maybe it's not important. The poet's live performance has its problems too, and limits the poem by directing us towards one interpretation, when the poem itself might actually possess several. But especially in the case of more difficult poems, the poet sometimes knows the line's *fullest* sense. Alas, not all semantic and tonal subtlety can be teased out through close reading alone, and sometimes the horse's mouth is the only way we can ever hear it.

Exile's End

You will do the very last thing.
Wait then for a noise in the chest,
between depth charge and gong,
like the seadoors slamming on the car deck.
Wait for the white noise and then cold astern.

Gaze down over the rim of the enormous lamp.
Observe the skilled frenzy of the physicians,
a nurse's bald patch, blood. These will blur,
as sure as you've forgotten the voices
of your childhood friends, or your toys.

Or, you may note with mild surprise,
your name. For the face they now cover
is a stranger's and it always has been.
Turn away. We commend you to the light,
Where all reliable accounts conclude.

Last words

This fifteen-line poem is a chilling affair, in which the speaker(s) provide us with a vision of our own deaths or – if we choose to read the poem as 'confessional' – the poet prophesies his own with alarming accuracy. The first line is a masterpiece of understated intensity. When else would we do the last thing? And what will that thing be – a breath, a cry, the rehearsal of a memory, an attempt to issue one last instruction? Whatever it is, that was your final improvisation. Thereafter all uncertainty and choice is gone, and we are given up to an inevitable sequence of events. It sounds as if the voice is delivering commands, but the imperative mood is really just explaining procedure: this is how it goes.

In all this terror we might forget the title is a *positive* one: *exile's end* is a homecoming. The first stanza begins the sea-journey, crossing the Styx in the big car ferry of souls. The *white noise* (which you'll know now as Donaghy-code for 'the great beyond') is the rising sound of our human receptive frequencies being tuned out, and the *cold astern*, I think, the cold of the body we're leaving behind. When the brain is starved of oxygen we get the proprioceptive hallucinations we call 'out-of-body experiences'. We're not *actually* floating above ourselves, but the neural connections that allow us to identify with our own bodies have been shut down. And then all blurs and disappears; we realize even our own name is a 'memory' that can be lost like any other. Perhaps the coldest line is *For the face they now cover / is a stranger's and it always has been*. In our living, we knew others, of course – but did we ever recognize ourselves? Who *were* we to us? We were no one, and only assumed this persona, this mask, for a play that has now ended.

Commend you to the light is something like 'we give you into the trust of the light' – where, it's implied, we will be finally safe. God knows we haven't been safe here. The phrase *where all reliable accounts conclude* simply says that beyond this threshold no stories can be brought back, at least none you can trust; but there is also a nice guilty Catholic hint of 'debts paid' in *accounts* – what Shakespeare would call *quietus*. A few claim to have returned, to have turned back from the light and found their way into their bodies, heads and minds again – but those who claim they went further are liars. This is the event horizon of our existence.

Beyond this we pass into . . . *What* kind of home, what kind of non-exile? And who are the *we*? They are our ferrymen, and perhaps not 'we' as in something composed of individuated souls, but something that merely cannot consider itself alone or singular. To which we can now be reconnected, and within which blissfully anonymized. Your exile *was* you.